Bhishma Nirvana

Nilesh Nilkanth Oak

Bhima LLC

ISBN-13: 978-0983034414

ISBN-10: 0983034419

Cover Design: Rupa Bhaty

Editing: Stephanie Ellison

Printed in the United States of America.

To

Baba
Bhaskar Padmanabh Sahasrabudhe
(13 Dec 1935 – 23 Dec 2015)

Bhishma dedicated his life to Dharma
Baba dedicated his life to Nirāmayakalpa™

Both passed away one day after the winter solstice

ACKNOWLEDGEMENTS

Ashwini, my wife, who cheered me up through my writer's block, read and re-read drafts of this book and gave crisp modifications.

Ms. Rupa Bhaty for designing the cover, multiple times, and Ms.. Stephanie Ellison for editing.

Abhi Shivadas and Chrystina Elle Passanisi for discussions and feedback.

Late Shri Prabhakar Phadnis (Appa) for being the devil's advocate.

The influence of Acharya Vinoba Bhave, Sir Karl Popper, and Joseph Campbell has served me well through my journey, and my ongoing studies of Shad-darshanas (Nyaya-Samkhya-Yoga-Vaisheshika-Purva and Uttar Mimansa) have allowed me to visualize the depth of Indic traditions of experimentation, science, and logic, and their untapped potential.

The views represented in this book are my own and not necessarily of those who have been kind to me, directly and indirectly, in this endeavor.

BHARAT is REBORN, as its most famous son, Lord Rama, has finally found a throne on world's timeline! And it is an open challenge from Nilesh Nilkanth Oak to the world to try and dethrone Lord Rama from that throne if they think they are intellectually up to the task.

--

It was a fascinating ride. The pictures helped enormously. It is funny, logical, unapologetic, interesting, thought-provoking, and most importantly, it requires a higher amount of reader participation. This is not a book for reading before bed or in a leisurely mood. This book is best read with a pen and a paper nearby.

--

The book is gripping, fascinating and it is hard to put it down.

--

I had a wonderful evening today explaining to my family how the 24-hour day, the 7-day week, the names of the weekdays, the sequence of weekday names, are all based on a system founded on logic of astronomy observations. And the week had an Out-of-India migration just like the Zero! So next time some AIT-Nazi talks you down, ask him what weekday it is! Nilesh ji, a big thank you to you, Sudarshan Bharadwaj and Shri Suhas Gurjar.

--

The book is excellent. I also enjoyed the last appendix on the "origins of weekday names and division." It seemed like a relief when I reached the appendix but ended up re-reading it in order to fully comprehend the gist of it.

--

Thank you so much for the work you have done to unearth the timelines of Ramayana. Reading the book gives me Goosebumps. I never had such an experience before. Hindus were blamed for not keeping track of time. Your research disproves it totally, clearly showing how the use of motion of celestial bodies serves as the ultimate timekeeper.

Praise for
"When did the Mahabharata War happen?
The Mystery of Arundhati"

You have done a great job. I requested astronomers to consider if Arundhati had gone ahead of Vasisth in 1971, when I published "Swayambhu." But nobody cared. You are the first to do the great job!
- Dr. P V Vartak (Author of "Swayambhu" & "Wastav Ramayana")
--

Grueling and unfaltering logic
--

I have to thank you for being the cause for a quantum leap in my own knowledge of general astronomy as well as Hindu astronomy / calendrical systems over a very short span of time. In some ways the effect of your book has some parallels with Rajiv Malhotra's "Being Different," though in a very different context. RM never intended his book as a primer on Dharma/Hinduism - but nevertheless it introduced many aspects of Dharma in a light which would be new even to a practitioner. Similarly, even though I am sure you never intended your book to act as an exploration of key astronomical principles and Vedic astronomy, that has definitely been a key side benefit, at least from my perspective.
--

Your rigorous methodology was simply a pleasure to read and that got me started off on my efforts to dabble in archeoastronomy. Please accept my best compliments on such a wonderful book.
--

"Indology" has been populated by linguists and my respect for their work has gone down by several notches when I look at the shoddy assumptions many are prone to make. Science and rigor the way Nilesh Oak has used seems to be unknown to these Indologists. I bet that not one of those horse bone chewers can understand what Archeo-astronomy means. Their awareness extends to looking at Archeo-asses and saying it was not Equus caballus.

Contents

1

Why write a book on Bhishma-Nirvana?

"Why do I write books? Why do I think? Why should I be passionate? Because things could be different, they could be made better."
-   Zygmunt Bauman

Before I published my first book, "When did the Mahabharata war happen? The mystery of Arundhati," there were more than 130 different claims for the year of the Mahabharta war. These claims ranged from 7300 BCE through 500 BCE. Only one of them could be true, since the other plausible scenario was that none of them could be true. I proved why 5561 BCE is the only possible date for the year of Mahabharata war.

In a scientific endeavor, all claims, even well tested and validated or accepted by mainstream as true are still tentative and open to falsification. In fact, science understands that all our existing theories and claims are one data (evidence) point away from falsification.

Multiple Claims for the Year of Mahabharata War

Many researchers were repeating the traditional and dogmatic belief of 3102 BCE +/-200 years and claiming it as their own. Others were repeating claims of past researchers and claiming them as their own by boasting that they had tested and validated these claims. Additional researchers were putting forward new claims, not being satisfied with existing claims, and were tauting these claims, so arrived, to be the final word on the chronology of the Mahabharata war.

Majority of these researchers have shown not even an inclination of scientific methodology in arriving at their claims. I realized the urgent need to identify and to eliminate superficial and manipulative claims. This was not an easy task because these researchers had used differing sets of evidence (arbitrary or selective) and different theories (multiple conflicting theories by same researcher), and they had deliberately avoided evidence that would have falsified their claims instantaneously. They had presented their works in ways that made it difficult to critique and compare specific claims with those of other researchers. Since they lacked scientific acumen, the only recourse they had was to claim their works, dogmatically, as the final word on the subject, and thus refused to respond to the criticism and refused to participate in debates. This had resulted in 130+ claims, where each researcher considered his claim to be the only truth but refused to respond to criticism of their works.

Separating the Genuine from the Pseudo

I wondered if I could develop a framework that Mahabharata enthusiasts can understand and use it to identify <u>superficial and manipulative claims</u> – specifically those that employed only selective or arbitrary sets of evidence, or those who employed multiple conflicting theories to arrive at their claims, or those who had not included specific evidence that would have instantaneously falsified these claims. I also wondered if the same framework can be used to identify claims that could be considered valid, albeit tentative, based on objective testing and logical reasoning.

The logic of scientific methodology has numerous aspects. I listed key aspects of the logic of scientific discovery as follows:

1. Consistency of a theory
2. Deductive reasoning
3. Clear and crisp statement of a theory
4. Insistence on objective testing
5. Insistence on testing all relevant evidence, both supporting

2

and conflicting the theory
6. Emphasis on corroboration and falsification, rather than "proving" and "disproving"
7. A revolutionary theory should lead to growth of knowledge

I selected following five specific elements to build my framework.

1. Evidence
2. Testability
3. Consistency of a theory
4. Corroboration and falsification
5. Growth of knowledge

Grains & chaff separation Matrix™

I developed a framework and named it "Grains & chaff separation matrix™".

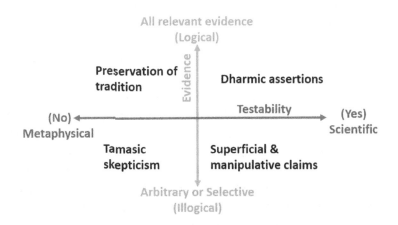

The lower end of the vertical axis of "evidence" is defined by "arbitrary or selective evidence" and the upper end of it is defined by "all relevant evidence." The horizontal axis of "testability" is defined by discrete definitions (yes or no). These simple criteria allow us to place any claim into one of the four categories (quadrants).

A research effort that focuses on preservation of ancient narratives, without any concern for testing them to check if they are valid or not, can be described as "metaphysical" and "logical." This **"Preservation of tradition"** is a critical function, and only because of the hard work of numerous individuals, our ancient heritage remains preserved for our benefit.

A research effort that focuses on analyzing all relevant evidence, in the light of a specific theory, and is concerned with proposing a theory in such a fashion so that all evidence becomes testable, can be described as "scientific" and "logical." **"Dharmic assertions"** is the desired approach and thus worthy of imitation. This is a rare occurrence, involves lot of hard work and luck. If successful, such efforts lead to revolutions.

A research effort that has semblance of "testability" due to its comprehension of the need for testability, but otherwise lacks the rationality of including "all relevant evidence", can be described as "illogical" and "testable." **"Speculative & manipulative claims"** is an undesirable approach. Unfortunately, most of research works on the dating of Mahabharata and Ramayana fall into this quadrant.

The remaining quadrant of **"Tamasic skepticism"** is characterized by metaphysical argumentation and lack of action. This includes invoking of specific references or observations from the ancient narratives that are not testable (and thus metaphysical), which are then employed to argue for the futility of research efforts or to claim non-historical nature of these ancient narratives. To enable these viewpoints, the emphasis is placed on descriptions, references, or observations from ancient narratives that are non-testable. The existence of such "non-testable" observations is employed to justify unauthenticity of numerous other observations that can be tested.

The framework can be easily modified to explore or represent other aspects of scientific methodology; however, the fundamentals remain the same. For example, if this framework is applied to the attitude of the researchers, then it can be represented as follows.

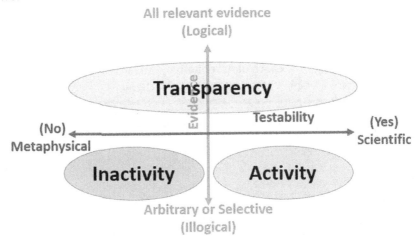

Epoch of Arundhati

The fact that one simple observation, now famous, the Arundhati-Vasistha (AV) observation, was not addressed by 99% of the researchers, and the fact that remaining 1% who acknowledged this observation had failed to empirically validate this observation led me to my own journey in determining the year of the Mahabharata war.

Bhishma (CE 2:31, GP 2:31)

या चैषा विश्रुता राजंस्त्रैलोक्ये साधुसंमता |
अरुन्धती तयाप्येष वसिष्ठः पृष्ठतः कृतः ||

The objective testing of this observation led me to the revolutionary inference that the Mahabharata war did not happen anytime after 4508 BCE! This was revolutionary because 95% + of all existing claims for the year of the Mahabharata war claimed a year that was after 4508 BCE. Thus, this single observation falsified instantaneously, 95% + of all existing claims. Readers and researchers with a solid comprehension of the scientific method recognized the revolutionary nature of this discovery.

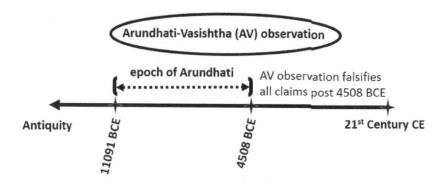

5561 BCE: The Year of the Mahabharta War

I validated not only AV observation, but also 200+ additional astronomy observations. Each observation was tested in an objective (and thus scientific) fashion in multiple ways via manual mathematical calculations and sophisticated astronomy software. I conclusively proved 5561 BCE as the year of the Mahabharata war.

I sent copies of my works to more than 50 individuals who had either proposed a timing of their own or had endorsed someone's claim for the chronology of the Mahabharata war. While two of them acknowledged the receipt of my book, there was no intellectual response from anyone either agreeing with my proposal or disagreeing with my proposal. After a few years went by, I would hear some of these researchers making feeble attempts to discredit my work. However, no researcher to date has come forward to debate his/her claim against my claim of 5561 BCE. I should mention that the claim for 5561 BCE as the year of the Mahabharata war was originally made by Dr. P. V. Vartak, sometime in the 1980s.

5561 BCE: The Planetary Evidence

I explained multiple descriptions of all distinguishable planets from the Mahabharata text for the very first time and so were the descriptions for the phases and positions of the moon, through the 18 days of the war. I solved the unsolvable problem of "vakri" motions of Mars and Jupiter. I also explained each instance of the retrograde motions of the planets – Jupiter, Saturn, Mars, Venus and Mercury – as described in the Mahabharata text.

My Theory of "Visual Observations of the Sky"

As a scientific theory, my theory met with great success. All other Mahabharata researchers have failed miserably on this count of scientific theory, notwithstanding their claims.

A revolutionary theory is defined by its ability to do the following:

1. Preserve the successes of previous theories
2. Explain observations not explained by previous theories
3. Make new predictions

My theory succeeded on all three counts and went beyond these three requirements. Before going into these details, it would be useful to mention some of the new and key predictions of my theory:

1. Duration of 98 days for Bhishma on the bed of arrows before he passed away
2. A definition for "vakri" (i.e., oblique motion across the ecliptic) motions of planets that is different than what we interpret as "vakri" (i.e., retrograde) motion of planets in modern Indian astronomy
3. 5525 BCE as the year for the flooding and destruction of Dwarka

4. Identification of "retrograde" motions and descriptions of planets. This prediction was necessitated by my original theory in explaining "vakri" motion of planets.
5. Hydrology and geology profile of the Sarasvati river at the time of the Mahabharata war

The ability of a theory to make novel predictions by itself is considered a great success of the theory. It does not matter if the predictions come out correct or not. This is because even if a prediction can not be validated by experimentation or evidence, it still leads to the growth of knowledge. It is then doubly fortunate that not only did my theory lead to numerous novel predictions, but it also led to empirical validation of these predictions. For example, predictions 1, 2, and 4 were validated by additional astronomy and chronology evidence of Mahabharata text, and predictions 3 and 5 were validated by oceanography, geology, geophysics, climatology, and hydrology evidence identified in recent years (1980-2018).

Preserving successes of past theories, explaining observations and phenomenon not explained by past theories, making novel predictions that are objectively testable, and to top it off, validation of these novel prediction by empirical evidence goes a long way in establishing the scientific basis of 5561 BCE as the year of the Mahabharata war.

Virtual Silence of Mahabharata Researchers

Many readers ask me the reason for the virtual silence of other Mahabharata researchers. I want to tell them that this is not a unique phenomenon. All revolutionary theories are ignored in the beginning with the hope that they never gain traction and are hopefully forgotten. The other reason these revolutionary theories are ignored because those who want to challenge these theories find it hard, if not impossible, to challenge them and to refute them.

The inability of Mahabharata researchers to challenge my work is not surprising. There are a few researchers who did attempt to challenge my claim, mostly with the borrowed claims of other re-searchers. The attempts backfired as it led to exposure of not only faulty understanding of their methodology, but also revealed their superficial knowledge of Mahabharata evidence. Their attempts to criticize my claim showed their lack of inferential acumen, as well as their ignorance about Mahabharta evidence. Thus, their efforts made my claim even stronger than before while their own claims appeared more ridiculous. What could be the secret sauce that led to this consistent outcome? The name of it is "Astronomy poison pill."

Astronomy Poison Pill

Astronomy poison pill (APP) is a fact, objectively testable, that creates a crisp, clean, rational, and scientific shield of extreme mathematical certainty, against dogmatic, skeptical or superficial/manipulative claims for the chronology of India's ancient narratives, and in turn for the chronology of ancient Indian history.

My work resulted in a series of 'poison pills.' The most potent 'poison pill' is the now-famous Arundhati-Vasishtha (AV) observation from the second adhyaya of Bhishma parva of the Mahabharata text. This single observation and its scientific testing disproved all existing claims for the chronology of the Mahabharata war. This poison pill disproves, instantaneously, any claim for the chronology of Mahabharata war that falls after 4508 BCE.

Planting Seeds and Removing Weeds

Research efforts leading to growth of knowledge in any field are equivalent to development and tending of a beautiful garden. The efforts include creative and destructive elements. Searching exhaustively for all relevant evidence, exploring alternate translations of textual evidence, exploration of multiple methods to test them objectively, formulation of a theory that is consistent, and simple, objective, and testing in an objective/rigorous fashion are the creative elements of this process. This is analogous to the

9

making of flower beds, planting of seeds, and watering them.

The destructive process involves identification of claims that are based on pseudo-scientific methods, claims that refuse to be tested against critical evidence, claims that avoid its falsification by only sticking to arbitrary and selective evidence and claims that are made to survive by deliberately explaining away crucial evidence as opposed to explaining the evidence in the context of the theory. This is analogous to the removal of weeds from the garden.

There are more than 130 specific claims by those many researchers for the chronology of the Mahabharata war. Let's classify them using "Grains & chaff separation matrix^{TM}".

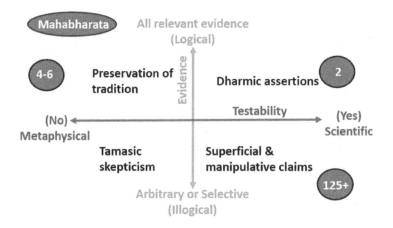

My research work, conducted over 20+ years, documented every identifiable piece of astronomy and chronology evidence from the Mahabharata text. The evidence amounted to more than 200 specific references/observations. Each of these observations were objectively tested, and this exercise lead to 5561 BCE as the year of the Mahabharata war. This effort in turn led to many novel predictions, and these predictions were tested against either internal evidence of the Mahabharata text or external evidence via multiple disciplines of science – hydrology, geology, geophysics, oceanography, seismology, climatology, genealogies of kings and sages, relative chronology of Rigveda mandalas, archaeology, anthropology, paleontology, and genetics. The claim for year 5561

BCE was corroborated and validated with flying colors by testable evidence from each of these disciplines of science.

The establishment, propagation, and further testing of the theory and the claim (5561 BCE), based on its scientific character, is analogous to the creation of a beautiful garden.

The framework also displayed the harsh reality of poor scholarship. Most of the researchers and their claims fell into "the superficial and manipulative" quadrant. These researchers employed only arbitrary and selective evidence. Thus, the framework allows us to identify these "superficial and manipulative claims." These fraudulent claims are the weeds and need to be recognized for what they are and must be removed. Astronomy poison pills kill these weeds.

Yet the weeds are strong, are entrenched deep in the popular psyche, and if we want to protect ourselves from future outbursts of such weeds, we must comprehend the potency of astronomy poison pills.

This book is written to explain the potency of two additional poison pills that emerged from the post Mahabharata war event of Bhishma-nirvana.

2

Evidence of Bhishma-nirvana

*"Facts are stubborn things; and whatever may be our wishes, our
inclinations, or the dictates of our passions, they cannot alter the
state of facts and evidence."*
-    John Adams

Bhishma is one of the key personalities from the Mahabharata.
The Mahabharata text preserves for us the descriptions of his activities. He fought reluctantly on the side of Duryodhana during
the Mahabharata war. He was one of the most powerful warriors
of his time. We will restrict our narration to the happenings that
began with the Mahabharata war and ended with the passing away
of Bhishma.

Bhishma was the supreme commander on Duryodhana's side
and fought for the first 10 days of the war. He fell in the battlefield, on the 10th day of the war, pierced by arrows. As Bhishma
fell, his body was held above the ground by the shafts of arrows.
When all gathered around him, Bhishma told them that his head
hung because of no support. Arjuna gave Bhishma a pillow of
arrows, befitting a warrior.

The war continued for additional 8 days and ended with the
defeat of Duryodhana by Bhima. That very night, Ashwatthma
killed the sons of Draupadi and many other warriors of the Pandava side. Bhima and Arjuna humbled Ashwatthama the next
day. On this day, the Kuru women arrived at the battlefield in
search of the dead bodies of their beloved.

Yudhishthira arranged the fire rites for the dead and then left
for the bank of Ganga, along with many others. He stayed on the
bank of river Ganga for a month and then returned to Hastinapur.

Yudhishtira arrived in Hastinapur, along with his brothers,
Dhritarastra, Krishna, and others. Yudhishthira was crowned a

king, and he assigned various administrative posts to specific individuals, assigned palaces to his brothers, and honored Krishna. Krishna reminded Yudhishthira to go and visit Bhishma, who was lying on the bed of arrows, at Kurukshetra.

Yudhisthira immediately left for Kurukshetra along with his brothers, Krishna, Satyaki, Yuyutsu, Kripacharya, Sanjaya and others. They arrived at Kuruskshetra and met Bhishma. It is on this day that Krishna told Bhishma that Bhishma had 56 additional days left to live, i.e., the day of winter solstice was 56 days away in the future.

Yudhisthira continued to visit Bhishma during the day for the next six days and he returned to Hastinapura for the night. On the sixth day, Bhishma recited "Vishnu-Sahasra-naama" to all present and then asked Yudhishthira to return to Hastinapura and return to Bhishma only when the sun turned north, i.e., only after the day of winter solstice.

Yudhisthira left Bhishma and returned to Hastinapura, along with his brothers, his ministers, Krishna, Satyaki, Dhritarashtra, Gandhari and lived there for 50 nights.

When the sun had turned north, he visited Bhishma, along with his entourage and all preparations for Bhishma-nirvana. It is on this day that Bhishma left his body and became one with the universe.

The narrative of Bhishma-nirvana is so straightforward that one can only wonder what made all Mahabharata researchers of the past and present (no exception) blatantly ignore the clear evidence and concoct their foolish theories and illogical explanations. We will get to the bottom of this intellectual rot (can we still call it 'intellectual'!?). However, we must first set out the factual evidence of the Mahabharata text.

6+ References of Bhishma-nirvana

When I wrote my first book, I identified six specific references that are sufficient to explain the entire 92+ days long duration of Bhishma on the bed of arrows.

23+ References of Bhishma-nirvana

When I began discussing this evidence with other Mahabharata researchers, they began accusing me of misinformation, and tried twisting the interpretation of these six specific observations related to Bhishma-nirvana. In responding to their specific objections, I extracted additional chronology and narrative references to falsify their misinterpretations. These amounted to 23 references. These 23 references are also part of my first book. While I was successful in falsifying their misinterpretations, they did not give up, and continued to come up with juvenile and illogical objections against my assertion of '92-plus-day-long duration of Bhishma on the bed of arrows.'

These researchers thought that they were objecting to my assertion. However, they were really objecting to the internal evidence of the Mahabharata text. Not surprisingly, the Mahabharata text supplied me with ample evidence to counter their illogical objections. The result of this endeavor led to many more than 23 observations for Bhishma-nirvana. They are presented in this book.

61+ References of Bhishma-nirvana

The evidence can be analyzed by broadly classifying it into two categories of (1) chronology evidence and (2) astronomy evidence, and then testing it in the context of (3) background knowledge of fundamental and applied astronomy.

Combining the chronology evidence with astronomy evidence allows us to set constraints on the events of Bhishma-nirvana. Interpretation of astronomy evidence, along with the constraints and duration of Bhishma on the bed of arrows allows us to estimate the epoch of Bhishma-nirvana. The evidence also enables us to perform sensitivity analysis on the epoch of Bhishma-nirvana that produces a robust time interval for the Bhishma-nirvana.

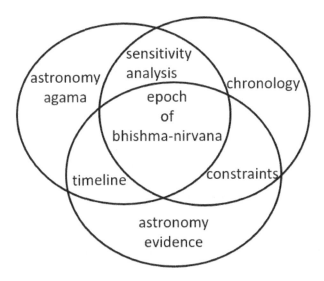

We will begin with chronology evidence.

3

Chronology Evidence

"What can be asserted without evidence can be dismissed without evidence."
- Christopher Hitchens

The Mahabharata text contains enormous evidence related to the chronology narrative of Bhishma-nirvana. The linear narration of events that begin with the fall of Bhishma on the 10th day of the war, runs through Bhishma, Drona, Karna, Shalya, Sauptic, Stri, Shanti, and Anushasan parvas, leading to the day of Bhishma-nirvana.

I had begun with six quantitative and chronological references for Bhishma-nirvana and thought they were crisp and clean, and more than sufficient to conclusively establish the duration of Bhishma on the bed of arrows. To my amazement, I underestimated the extent of delusion, intellectual rot and dishonesty, and sheer laziness of the Mahabharata researchers. These researchers were either incompetent or outright frauds. They were incapable and unwilling to reach the factual conclusions even when I made available overwhelming amount of evidence from the Mahabharata text.

It was then interesting to note that as they raised trival sounding objections against the factual timeline of Bhishma-nirvana and as I read and re-read the Mahabharata text, trying to respond to their objections, I unearthed enormous additional evidence. If I must quote all of it, it would amount to quoting entire "parvas" of the Mahabharata text. For brevity, we will limit ourselves to minimum necessary evidence that clearly outlines the narration of Bhishma-nirvana in a quantitative fashion, and one that clearly states the sequence of events.

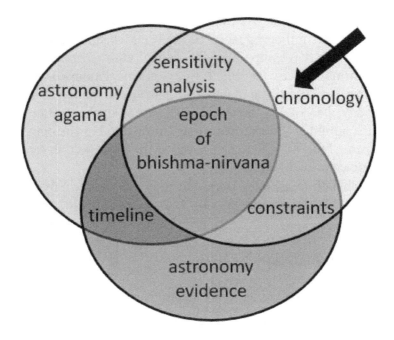

3.1 Fall of Bhishma to Bhishma-nirvana

Bhishma fell in the battle on the 10th day of the war and since then was lying on the bed of arrows until the day of winter solstice.

The war continued for an additional 8 days (total of 18 days), and by the time the war was over, Bhishma was already on the bed of arrows for 9 days.

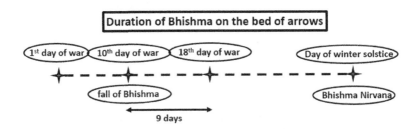

The war appeared to have ended with the falling of Duryodhana during the Duryodhana-Bhima gada-yuddha, on the

18th day of the war. Ashwatthama asked fallen Duryodhana to make him the military general of the Kaurava side and then went to the Pandava camp at night, along with Kripacharya and Kritavarma, where he killed five sons of Draupadi, Dhrista-dyumna, Shikhandi and many other warriors of Pandava side. The next day, i.e., the day after the 18th day of the war, Bhima and Arjuna humbled Ashwatthama and returned to Hastinapura. This is when all the Kuru women arrived at the battlefield in search of the bodies of their loved ones.

Yudhishthira asked Vidura, Dhaumya, Sanjaya, Yuyutsu, Indrasen, and others to plan for the preta-karma of the fallen warriors.

Stri (CE 26:24-26, GP 26:24-26)

एवमुक्तो महाप्राज्ञः कुन्तीपुत्रो युधिष्ठिरः |
आदिदेश सुधर्माणं धौम्यं सूतं च सञ्जयम् ||२४||

विदुरं च महाबुद्धिं युयुत्सुं चैव कौरवम् |
इन्द्रसेनमुखांश्चैव भृत्यान्सूतांश्च सर्वशः ||२५||

भवन्तः कारयन्त्वेषां प्रेतकार्याणि सर्वशः |
यथा चानाथवत्किञ्चिच्छरीरं न विनश्यति ||२६||

Vidura and others conducted the preta-kriya accordingly, and the place became bright with "preta-kriya" of thousands of dead warriors.

Stri (CE 26:27-38, GP 26:27-38)

शासनाद्धर्मराजस्य क्षत्ता सूतश्च सञ्जयः |
सुधर्मा धौम्यसहित इन्द्रसेनादयस्तथा ||२७||

चन्दनागुरुकाष्ठानि तथा कालीयकान्युत |
घृतं तैलं च गन्धांश्च क्षौमाणि वसनानि च ||२८||

समाहृत्य महार्हाणि दारूणां चैव सञ्चयान् |
रथांश्च मृदितांस्तत्र नानाप्रहरणानि च ||२९||

चिताः कृत्वा प्रयत्नेन यथामुख्यान्नराधिपान् |
दाहयामासुरव्यग्रा विधिदृष्टेन कर्मणा ||३०||

दुर्योधनं च राजानं भ्रातृंश्चास्य शताधिकान् |
शल्यं शलं च राजानं भूरिश्रवसमेव च ||३१||

जयद्रथं च राजानमभिमन्युं च भारत |
दौःशासनिं लक्ष्मणं च धृष्टकेतुं च पार्थिवम् ||३२||

बृहन्तं सोमदत्तं च सृञ्जयांश्च शताधिकान् |
राजानं क्षेमधन्वानं विराटद्रुपदौ तथा ||३३||

शिखण्डिनं च पाञ्चाल्यं धृष्टद्युम्नं च पार्षतम् |
युधामन्युं च विक्रान्तमुत्तमौजसमेव च ||३४||

कौसल्यं द्रौपदेयांश्च शकुनिं चापि सौबलम् |
अचलं वृषकं चैव भगदत्तं च पार्थिवम् ||३५||

कर्णं वैकर्तनं चैव सहपुत्रममर्षणम् |
केकयांश्च महेष्वासांस्त्रिगर्तांश्च महारथान् ||३६||

घटोत्कचं राक्षसेन्द्रं बकभ्रातरमेव च |

अलम्बुसं च राजानं जलसन्धं च पार्थिवम् ||३७||

अन्यांश्च पार्थिवान्नाजञ्शतशोऽथ सहस्रशः |
घृतधाराहु तैर्दीप्तैः पावकैः समदाहयन् ||३८||

Pitru-medha began for key warriors and sounds of sama-gana could be heard. The night was filled with the sounds of sama-gana and the wailing of kuru women.

Stri (CE 26:39-40, GP 26:39-40)

पितृमेधाश्च केषाञ्चिदवर्तन्त महात्मनाम् |
सामभिश्चाप्यगायन्त तेऽन्वशोच्यन्त चापरैः ||३९||

साम्नामृचां च नादेन स्त्रीणां च रुदितस्वनैः |
कश्मलं सर्वभूतानां निशायां समपद्यत ||४०||

Vidura ordered "preta-kriya" for the bodies of numerous unknown warriors who had arrived from distant places to participate in the war.

Stri (CE 26:42-43, GP 26:42-43)

ये चाप्यनाथास्तत्रासन्नानादेशसमागताः |
तांश्च सर्वान्समानाय्य राशीन्कृत्वा सहस्रशः ||४२||

चित्वा दारुभिरव्यग्रः प्रभूतैः स्नेहतापितैः |
दाहयामास विदुरो धर्मराजस्य शासनात् ||४३||

After completing "preta-kriya," Yudhishthira left for the bank of Ganga along with Dhritarashtra and others.

Stri (CE 26:44, GP 26:44)

कारयित्वा क्रियास्तेषां कुरुराजो युधिष्ठिरः |
धृतराष्ट्रं पुरस्कृत्य गङ्गामभिमुखोऽगमत् ||४४||

They arrived on the bank of river Ganga and then began the "preta-kritya" by entering the waters of the Ganga river.

Stri (CE 27:1-2, GP 27:1-2)

ते समासाद्य गङ्गां तु शिवां पुण्यजनोचिताम् |
ह्रदिनीं वप्रसम्पन्नां महानूपां महावनाम् ||१||

भूषणान्युत्तरीयाणि वेष्टनान्यवमुच्य च |
ततः पितृणां पौत्राणां भ्रातृणां स्वजनस्य च ||२||

Yudhishthira invited the widows of Karna and along with them, performed "preta-kritya" for Karna and then came out of the water of the Ganga river to its bank.

Stri (CE 27:23-24, GP 27:23-24)

तत आनाययामास कर्णस्य सपरिच्छदम् |
स्त्रियः कुरुपतिर्धीमान्भातुः प्रेम्णा युधिष्ठिरः ||२३||

स ताभिः सह धर्मात्मा प्रेतकृत्यमनन्तरम् |
कृत्वोत्तार गङ्गायाः सलिलादाकुलेन्द्रियः ||२४||

Yudhishthira and the party thus completed "Preta-kritya" in the waters of river Ganga and then stayed on the bank of Ganga, seeking Atma-shuddhi, for a month.

Shanti (CE 1:1-2, GP 1:1-2)

कृतोदकास्ते सुहृदां सर्वेषां पाण्डुनन्दनाः |
विदुरो धृतराष्ट्रश्च सर्वाश्च भरतस्त्रियः ||१||

तत्र ते सुमहात्मानो न्यवसन्कुरुनन्दनाः |
शौचं निवर्तयिष्यन्तो मासमेकं बहिः पुरात् ||२||

Sage Narada and sage Vyasa discussed relevant narrations and responded to questions of Yudhishthira. They spent about a month on the bank of the river Ganga. We will estimate this duration of a month in the most conservative fashion, realizing that the actual duration could be longer, but never shorter than, the most conservative estimate. As a most conservative estimate, we would assume this duration to be equal to the length of sidereal lunar month, i.e, ~27 days. This means that by the time Yudhishthira had completed his stay on the bank of the river Ganga, Bhishma was already on the bed of arrows for a minimum of (9 + 27) days.

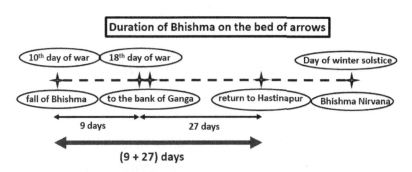

When Yudhishthir asked both sages to expound on the conflicting reality of following Dharma and administration of the kingdom, Vyasa suggested that it is better that Yudhishthira seek this counsel from Bhishma.

Shanti (CE 38:5-6, GP 37:5-6)

तमुवाच महातेजा व्यासो वेदविदां वरः |
नारदं समभिप्रेक्ष्य सर्वं जानन्पुरातनम् ||५||

श्रोतुमिच्छसि चेद्धर्मानखिलेन युधिष्ठिर |
प्रैहि भीष्मं महाबाहो वृद्धं कुरुपितामहम् ||६||

Vyasa added that Bhishma is an expert in the subject of subtleties of dharma and artha, and that Yudhishthira should approach Bhishma before the latter passes away.

Shanti (CE 38:16, GP 37:16)

स ते वक्ष्यति धर्मज्ञः सूक्ष्मधर्मार्थतत्त्ववित् |
तमभ्येहि पुरा प्राणान्स विमुञ्चति धर्मवित् ||१६||

Yudhishthira listened to this advice of sage Vyasa and decided to leave the bank of the river Ganga and traveled towards Hastina-pura and entered the city.

Shanti (CE 38:30, GP 37:30)

स तैः परिवृतो राजा नक्षत्रैरिव चन्द्रमाः |
धृतराष्ट्रं पुरस्कृत्य स्वपुरं प्रविवेश ह ||३०||

The residents of Hastinapura welcomed Yudhishthira and his entourage with great celebration.

Shanti (CE 38:31-49, GP 37:31-49)

प्रविविक्षुः स धर्मज्ञः कुन्तीपुत्रो युधिष्ठिरः |
अर्चयामास देवांश्च ब्राह्मणांश्च सहस्रशः ||३१||

23

ततो रथं नवं शुभ्रं कम्बलाजिनसंवृतम् |
युक्तं षोडशभिर्गोभिः पाण्डुरैः शुभलक्षणैः ||३२||

मन्त्रैरभ्यर्चितः पुण्यैः स्तूयमानो महर्षिभिः |
आरुरोह यथा देवः सोमोऽमृतमयं रथम् ||३३||

जग्राह रश्मीन्कौन्तेयो भीमो भीमपराक्रमः |
अर्जुनः पाण्डुरं छत्रं धारयामास भानुमत् ||३४||

ध्रियमाणं तु तच्छत्रं पाण्डुरं तस्य मूर्धनि |
शुशुभे तारकाराजसितमभ्रमिवाम्बरे ||३५||

चामरव्यजने चास्य वीरौ जगृहतुस्तदा |
चन्द्ररश्मिप्रभे शुभ्रे माद्रीपुत्रावलङ्कृते ||३६||

ते पञ्च रथमास्थाय भ्रातरः समलङ्कृताः |
भूतानीव समस्तानि राजन्ददृशिरे तदा ||३७||

आस्थाय तु रथं शुभ्रं युक्तमश्वैर्महाजवैः |
अन्वयात्पृष्ठतो राजन्युयुत्सुः पाण्डवाग्रजम् ||३८||

रथं हेममयं शुभ्रं सैन्यसुग्रीवयोजितम् |
सह सात्यकिना कृष्णः समास्थायान्वयात्कुरून् ||३९||

नरयानेन तु ज्येष्ठः पिता पार्थस्य भारत |
अग्रतो धर्मराजस्य गान्धारीसहितो ययौ ||४०||

कुरुस्त्रियश्च ताः सर्वाः कुन्ती कृष्णा च द्रौपदी |

यानैरुच्चावचैर्जग्मुर्विदुरेण पुरस्कृताः ||४१||

ततो रथाश्च बहुला नागाश्च समलङ्कृताः |
पादाताश्च हयाश्चैव पृष्ठतः समनुव्रजन् ||४२||

ततो वैतालिकैः सूतैर्मागधैश्च सुभाषितैः |
स्तूयमानो ययौ राजा नगरं नागसाह्वयम् ||४३||

तत्प्रयाणं महाबाहोर्बभूवाप्रतिमं भुवि |
आकुलाकुलमुत्सृष्टं हृष्टपुष्टजनान्वितम् ||४४||

अभियाने तु पार्थस्य नरैर्नगरवासिभिः |
नगरं राजमार्गश्च यथावत्समलङ्कृतम् ||४५||

पाण्डुरेण च माल्येन पताकाभिश्च वेदिभिः |
संवृतो राजमार्गश्च धूपनैश्च सुधूपितः ||४६||

अथ चूर्णैश्च गन्धानां नानापुष्पैः प्रियङ्गुभिः |
माल्यदामभिरासक्तै राजवेश्माभिसंवृतम् ||४७||

कुम्भाश्च नगरद्वारि वारिपूर्णा दृढा नवाः |
कन्याः सुमनसश्छागाः स्थापितास्तत्र तत्र ह ||४८||

तथा स्वलङ्कृतद्वारं नगरं पाण्डुनन्दनः |
स्तूयमानः शुभैर्वाक्यैः प्रविवेश सुहृद्वृतः ||४९||

Yudhishthira was coronated as a king.

Shanti (CE 40:1-22, GP 40:1-24)

ततः कुन्तीसुतो राजा गतमन्युर्गतज्वरः |
काञ्चने प्राङ्मुखो हृष्टो न्यषीदत्परमासने ||१||

तमेवाभिमुखौ पीठे सेव्यास्तरणसंवृते |
सात्यकिर्वासुदेवश्च निषीदतुररिंदमौ ||२||

मध्ये कृत्वा तु राजानं भीमसेनार्जुनावुभौ |
निषीदतुर्महात्मानौ श्लक्ष्णयोर्मणिपीठयोः ||३||

दान्ते शय्यासने शुभ्रे जाम्बूनदविभूषिते |
पृथापि सहदेवेन सहास्ते नकुलेन च ||४||

सुधर्मा विदुरो धौम्यो धृतराष्ट्रश्च कौरवः |
निषेदुर्ज्वलनाकारेष्वासनेषु पृथक्पृथक् ||५||

युयुत्सुः सञ्जयश्चैव गान्धारी च यशस्विनी |
धृतराष्ट्रो यतो राजा ततः सर्व उपाविशन् ||६||

तत्रोपविष्टो धर्मात्मा श्वेताः सुमनसोऽस्पृशत् |
स्वस्तिकानक्षतान्भूमिं सुवर्णं रजतं मणीन् ||७||

ततः प्रकृतयः सर्वाः पुरस्कृत्य पुरोहितम् |
ददृशुर्धर्मराजानमादाय बहु मङ्गलम् ||८||

पृथिवीं च सुवर्णं च रत्नानि विविधानि च |
आभिषेचनिकं भाण्डं सर्वसम्भारसम्भृतम् ||९||

काञ्चनौदुम्बरास्तत्र राजताः पृथिवीमयाः |
पूर्णकुम्भाः सुमनसो लाजा बर्हीषि गोरसाः ||१०||

शमीपलाशपुंनागाः समिधो मधुसर्पिषी |
सुव औदुम्बरः शङ्खास्तथा हेमविभूषिताः ||११||

दाशार्हेणाभ्यनुज्ञातस्तत्र धौम्यः पुरोहितः |
प्रागुदक्प्रवणां वेदीं लक्षणेनोपलिप्य ह ||१२||

व्याघ्रचर्मोत्तरे श्लक्ष्णे सर्वतोभद्र आसने |
दृढपादप्रतिष्ठाने हुताशनसमत्विषि ||१३||

उपवेश्य महात्मानं कृष्णां च द्रुपदात्मजाम् |
जुहाव पावकं धीमान्विधिमन्त्रपुरस्कृतम् ||१४||

अभ्यषिञ्चत्पतिं पृथ्व्याः कुन्तीपुत्रं युधिष्ठिरम् |
धृतराष्ट्रश्च राजर्षिः सर्वाः प्रकृतयस्तथा ||१५||

ततोऽनुवादयामासुः पणवानकदुन्दुभीः |
धर्मराजोऽपि तत्सर्वं प्रतिजग्राह धर्मतः ||१६||

पूजयामास तांश्चापि विधिवद्भूरिदक्षिणः |
ततो निष्कसहस्रेण ब्राह्मणान्स्वस्ति वाचयत् ||१७||

वेदाध्ययनसम्पन्नाञ्शीलवृत्तसमन्वितान् ||१७||

ते प्रीता ब्राह्मणा राजन्स्वस्त्यूचुर्जयमेव च |
हंसा इव च नर्दन्तः प्रशशंसुर्युधिष्ठिरम् ||१८||

युधिष्ठिर महाबाहो दिष्ट्या जयसि पाण्डव |
दिष्ट्या स्वधर्म प्राप्तोऽसि विक्रमेण महाद्युते ||१९||

दिष्ट्या गाण्डीवधन्वा च भीमसेनश्च पाण्डवः |
त्वं चापि कुशली राजन्माद्रीपुत्रौ च पाण्डवौ ||२०||

मुक्ता वीरक्षयादस्मात्सङ्ग्रामान्निहतद्विषः |
क्षिप्रमुत्तरकालानि कुरु कार्याणि पाण्डव ||२१||

ततः प्रत्यर्चितः सद्भिर्धर्मराजो युधिष्ठिरः |
प्रतिपेदे महद्राज्यं सुहृद्भिः सह भारत ||२२||

Yudhishthira took leave of his audience who attended his coronation ceremony and appointed Bhima as the Yuvaraj. He
appointed Vidura as his counselor, and assigned duties related to
collection of revenue as well as execution of administrative tasks
to Sanjaya. Yudhishthira assigned Nakula to all aspects of army
management and Arjuna as the military chief. He assigned
Dhaumya as his dharma counselor and Sahadeva as the head of
his personal security. He requested Vidura, Sanjaya and Yuyutsu
to take good care of Dhritarashtra and address the concerns of residents of Hastinapura and his kingdom.

Shanti (CE 41:1-18, GP 41:1-19)

अनुगम्य च राजानं यथेष्टं गम्यतामिति |
पौरजानपदान्सर्वान्विसृज्य कुरुनन्दनः ||८||
यौवराज्येन कौरव्यो भीमसेनमयोजयत् ||८||

मन्त्रे च निश्चये चैव षाड्गुण्यस्य च चिन्तने |

28

विदुरं बुद्धिसम्पन्नं प्रीतिमान्वै समादिशत् ॥९॥

कृताकृतपरिज्ञाने तथायव्ययचिन्तने ।
सञ्जयं योजयामास ऋद्धमृद्धैर्गुणैर्युतम् ॥१०॥

बलस्य परिमाणे च भक्तवेतनयोस्तथा ।
नकुलं व्यादिशद्राजा कर्मिणामन्ववेक्षणे ॥११॥

परचक्रोपरोधे च दृप्तानां चावमर्दने ।
युधिष्ठिरो महाराजः फल्गुनं व्यादिदेश ह ॥१२॥

द्विजानां वेदकार्येषु कार्येष्वन्येषु चैव हि ।
धौम्यं पुरोधसां श्रेष्ठं व्यादिदेश परन्तपः ॥१३॥

सहदेवं समीपस्थं नित्यमेव समादिशत् ।
तेन गोप्यो हि नृपतिः सर्वावस्थो विशां पते ॥१४॥

यान्यान्मन्यद्योग्यांश्च येषु येष्विह कर्मसु ।
तांस्तांस्तेष्वेव युयुजे प्रीयमाणो महीपतिः ॥१५॥

विदुरं सञ्जयं चैव युयुत्सुं च महामतिम् ।
अब्रवीत्परवीरघ्नो धर्मात्मा धर्मवत्सलः ॥१६॥

उत्थायोत्थाय यत्कार्यमस्य राज्ञः पितुर्मम ।
सर्वं भवद्भिः कर्तव्यमप्रमत्तैर्यथातथम् ॥१७॥

पौरजानपदानां च यानि कार्याणि नित्यशः ।
राजानं समनुज्ञाप्य तानि कार्याणि धर्मतः ॥१८॥

Yudhishthira conducted "Shraddha-karma" along with Dhritarashtra and then honored Krishna. He assigned, at the request of Dhritarashtra, the palace of Duryodhana to Bhimasen, Dushasana's palace to Arjuna, Durmashana's palace to Nakula and Durmukha's palace to Sahadeva. Yuyutsu, Vidura, Sanjaya, Sudhrama and Dhaumya continued with their existing residences.

Shanti (CE 44:6-14, GP 44:6-14)

ततो दुर्योधनगृहं प्रासादैरुपशोभितम् |
बहु रत्नसमाकीर्णं दासीदाससमाकुलम् ||६||

धृतराष्ट्राभ्यनुज्ञातं भ्रात्रा दत्तं वृकोदरः |
प्रतिपेदे महाबाहु र्मन्दरं मघवानिव ||७||

यथा दुर्योधनगृहं तथा दुःशासनस्य च |
प्रासादमालासंयुक्तं हेमतोरणभूषितम् ||८||
दासीदाससुसम्पूर्णं प्रभूतधनधान्यवत् |
प्रतिपेदे महाबाहु रर्जुनो राजशासनात् ||९||

दुर्मर्षणस्य भवनं दुःशासनगृहाद्वरम् |
कुबेरभवनप्रख्यं मणिहेमविभूषितम् ||१०||

नकुलाय वराहार्हाय कर्शिताय महावने |
ददौ प्रीतो महाराज धर्मराजो युधिष्ठिरः ||११||

दुर्मुखस्य च वेश्माग्र्यं श्रीमत्कनकभूषितम् |
पूर्णं पद्मदलाक्षीणां स्त्रीणां शयनसङ्कुलम् ||१२||

प्रददौ सहदेवाय सततं प्रियकारिणे |
मुमुदे तच्च लब्ध्वा स कैलासं धनदो यथा ||१३||

 युयुत्सुर्विदुरश्चैव सञ्जयश्च महाद्युतिः |
सुधर्मा चैव धौम्यश्च यथास्वं जग्मुरालयान् ||१४||

Krishna went to the palace of Arjuna along with Satyaki and spent the night. When they were well rested for the night, they woke up in the morning, became ready, and then went to see Yudhishthira.

Shanti (CE 44:15-16, GP 44:15-16)

सह सात्यकिना शौरिरर्जुनस्य निवेशनम् |
विवेश पुरुषव्याघ्रो व्याघ्रो गिरिगुहामिव ||१५||

तत्र भक्षान्नपानैस्ते समुपेताः सुखोषिताः |
सुखप्रबुद्धा राजानमुपतस्थुर्युधिष्ठिरम् ||१६||

Yudhishthira welcomed Krishna, asked Krishna of his well-being, and yet he noticed that Krishna was in some deep thought.

Shanti (CE 45:17-20, GP 45:17-20)

सुखेन ते निशा कच्चिद्व्युष्टा बुद्धिमतां वर |
कच्चिज्ज्ञानानि सर्वाणि प्रसन्नानि तवाच्युत ||१७||

तव ह्याश्रित्य तां देवीं बुद्धिं बुद्धिमतां वर |
वयं राज्यमनुप्राप्ताः पृथिवी च वशे स्थिता ||१८||

भवत्प्रसादाद्भगवंस्त्रिलोकगतिविक्रम |

जयः प्राप्तो यशश्चाग्र्यं न च धर्माच्च्युता वयम् ||१९||
तं तथा भाषमाणं तु धर्मराजं युधिष्ठिरम् |
नोवाच भगवान्किञ्चिद्ध्यानमेवान्वपद्यत ||२०||

When Yudhishthira asked Krishna as to what he was thinking about, Krishna responded that Bhishma who is lying on the bed of arrows is thinking of him and therefore he is also thinking of Bhishma. Krishna reminded Yudhishthira that Bhishma, who was lying on the bed of arrows, would soon pass away and that Yudhishthira should approach Bhishma and ask all the questions.

Shanti (CE 46:11, GP 46:11)

शरतल्पगतो भीष्मः शाम्यन्निव हुताशनः |
मां ध्याति पुरुषव्याघ्रस्ततो मे तद्गतं मनः ||११||

Shanti (CE 46:20-23, GP 46:20-23)

तस्मिन्हि पुरुषव्याघ्रे कर्मभिः स्वैर्दिवं गते |
भविष्यति मही पार्थ नष्टचन्द्रेव शर्वरी ||२०||
तद्युधिष्ठिर गाङ्गेयं भीष्मं भीमपराक्रमम् |
अभिगम्योपसङ्गृह्य पृच्छ यत्ते मनोगतम् ||२१||

चातुर्वेद्यं चातुर्होत्रं चातुराश्रम्यमेव च |
चातुर्वर्ण्यस्य धर्मं च पृच्छैनं पृथिवीपते ||२२||

तस्मिन्नस्तमिते भीष्मे कौरवाणां धुरन्धरे |
ज्ञानान्यल्पीभविष्यन्ति तस्मात्त्वां चोदयाम्यहम् ||२३||

Yudhishthira agreed with the suggestion of Krishna and assented.

Shanti (CE 46:28-29, GP 46:28-29)

यतस्त्वनुग्रहकृता बुद्धिस्ते मयि माधव।
त्वामग्रतः पुरस्कृत्य भीष्मं पश्यामहे वयम् ॥२८॥

आवृते भगवत्यर्के स हि लोकान्गमिष्यति।
त्वद्दर्शनं महाबाहो तस्मादर्हति कौरवः ॥२९॥

Krishna asked Satyaki to have his chariot ready and Satyaki in turn asked Daruka to have the chariot ready.

Shanti (CE 46:31-32, GP 46:31-32)

श्रुत्वैतद्धर्मराजस्य वचनं मधुसूदनः।
पार्श्वस्थं सात्यकिं प्राह रथो मे युज्यतामिति ॥३१॥

सात्यकिस्तूपनिष्क्रम्य केशवस्य समीपतः।
दारुकं प्राह कृष्णस्य युज्यतां रथ इत्युत ॥३२॥

Day of Bhishma-nirvana and the Day of Winter Solstice

When King Janamejaya asked sage Vaishampayana about the timing of Bhishma-nirvana, Vaishampayana answered by stating that Bhishma passed away as soon as the sun turned north.

Shanti (CE 47:1-3, GP 47:1-3)

जनमेजय उवाच॥
शरतल्पे शयानस्तु भरतानां पितामहः।
कथमुत्सृष्टवान्देहं कं च योगमधारयत् ॥१॥

वैशम्पायन उवाच॥

शृणुष्वावहितो राजञ्शुचिर्भूत्वा समाहितः |
भीष्मस्य कुरुशार्दूल देहोत्सर्गं महात्मनः ||२||

निवृत्तमात्रे त्वयन उत्तरे वै दिवाकरे |
समावेशयदात्मानमात्मन्येव समाहितः ||३||

    Krishna and Satyaki boarded on one chariot while Yudhishthira and Arjuna on the second chariot. Bhima, Nakula, and Sahadeva boarded the third chariot while Kripacharya, Yuyutsu and Sanjaya boarded the fourth chariot.

Shanti (CE 47:68-72, GP 47:105-109)

विदित्वा भक्तियोगं तु भीष्मस्य पुरुषोत्तमः |
सहसोत्थाय संहृष्टो यानमेवान्वपद्यत ||६८||

केशवः सात्यकिश्चैव रथेनैकेन जग्मतुः |
अपरेण महात्मानौ युधिष्ठिरधनञ्जयौ ||६९||

भीमसेनो यमौ चोभौ रथमेकं समास्थितौ |
कृपो युयुत्सुः सूतश्च सञ्जयश्चापरं रथम्|||७०||

ते रथैर्नगराकारैः प्रयाताः पुरुषर्षभाः |
नेमिघोषेण महता कम्पयन्तो वसुन्धराम् ||७१||

ततो गिरः पुरुषवरस्तवान्विता; द्विजेरिताः पथि सुमनाः स शुश्रुवे |
कृताञ्जलिं प्रणतमथापरं जनं; स केशिहा मुदितमनाभ्यनन्दत ||७२||

    They soon arrived at Kurukshetra. The place was filled with hair, bones, and human skulls. They continued traveling to the location where Bhishma was lying on the bed of arrows.

Shanti (CE 48:1-6, GP 48:1-6)

ततः स च हृषीकेशः स च राजा युधिष्ठिरः |
कृपादयश्च ते सर्वे चत्वारः पाण्डवाश्च ह ||१||

रथैस्ते नगराकारैः पताकाध्वजशोभितैः |
ययुराशु कुरुक्षेत्रं वाजिभिः शीघ्रगामिभिः ||२||

तेऽवतीर्य कुरुक्षेत्रं केशमज्जास्थिसङ्कुलम् |
देहन्यासः कृतो यत्र क्षत्रियैस्तैर्महात्मभिः ||३||

गजाश्वदेहास्थिचयैः पर्वतैरिव सञ्चितम् |
नरशीर्षकपालैश्च शङ्खैरिव समाचितम् ||४||

चितासहस्रैर्निचितं वर्मशस्त्रसमाकुलम् |
आपानभूमिं कालस्य तदा भुक्तोज्झितामिव ||५||

भूतसङ्घानुचरितं रक्षोगणनिषेवितम् |
पश्यन्तस्ते कुरुक्षेत्रं ययुराशु महारथाः ||६||

Soon, they arrived near Bhishma, who was lying on the bank
of the Oghavati river, surrounded by many sages.

Shanti (CE 50:5-7, GP 50:5-7)

तथा यान्तौ तदा तात तावच्युतयुधिष्ठिरौ |
जग्मतुर्यत्र गाङ्गेयः शरतल्पगतः प्रभुः ||५||

ततस्ते ददृशुर्भीष्मं शरप्रस्तरशायिनम् |
स्वरश्मिजालसंवीतं सायंसूर्यमिवानलम् ||६||

35

उपास्यमानं मुनिभिर्देवैरिव शतक्रतुम् |
देशे परमधर्मिष्ठे नदीमोघवतीमनु ||७||

When they saw Bhishma, they came down from their chariots, still at a distance from Bhishma, and walked towards Bhishma and the sages, paid their obeisances to sages and Bhishma, and then sat down in a circle around Bhishma.

Shanti (CE 50:8-11, GP 50:8-11)

दूरादेव तमालोक्य कृष्णो राजा च धर्मराट् |
चत्वारः पाण्डवाश्चैव ते च शारद्वतादयः ||८||

अवस्कन्द्याथ वाहेभ्यः संयम्य प्रचलं मनः |
एकीकृत्येन्द्रियग्राममुपतस्थुर्महामुनीन् ||९||

अभिवाद्य च गोविन्दः सात्यकिस्ते च कौरवाः |
व्यासादींस्तानृषीन्पश्चाद्गाङ्गेयमुपतस्थिरे ||१०||

तपोवृद्धिं ततः पृष्ट्वा गाङ्गेयं यदुकौरवाः |
परिवार्य ततः सर्वे निषेदुः पुरुषर्षभाः ||११||

Krishna asked Bhishma about his health and told him the purpose of their visit. Krishna praised Bhishma as the person who knew itihasa, puranas, and dharma-shastra, and his skills at resolving doubts of others, and further requested him to remove the grief of Yudhishthira.

Shanti (CE 50:34-36, GP 50:36-38)

इतिहासपुराणं च कात्स्न्र्येन विदितं तव |
धर्मशास्त्रं च सकलं नित्यं मनसि ते स्थितम् ||३४||

ये च केचन लोकेऽस्मिन्नर्थाः संशयकारकाः |
तेषां छेत्ता नास्ति लोके त्वदन्यः पुरुषर्षभ ||३५||

स पाण्डवेयस्य मनःसमुत्थितं; नरेन्द्र शोकं व्यपकर्ष मेधया |
भवद्विधा ह्युत्तमबुद्धिविस्तरा; विमुह्यमानस्य जनस्य शान्तये ||३६||

Bhishma in turn praised Krishna, and Krishna told Bhishma that the latter's study and austerity is sufficient to reach moksha. It is now that on this day, Krishna told Bhishma that the latter had 56 more days to live, i.e., the day of winter solstice was about 56 days away into the future, and he again requested Bhishma to impart knowledge to Yudhishthira.

Shanti (CE 51:13-18, GP 51:13-18)

अहस्त्वं भीष्म मां द्रष्टुं तपसा स्वेन पार्थिव |
तव ह्युपस्थिता लोका येभ्यो नावर्तते पुनः ||१३||

पञ्चाशतं षट्च कुरुप्रवीर; शेषं दिनानां तव जीवितस्य |
ततः शुभैः कर्मफलोदयैस्त्वं; समेष्यसे भीष्म विमुच्य देहम् ||१४||

एते हि देवा वसवो विमाना; न्यास्थाय सर्वे ज्वलिताग्निकल्पाः |
अन्तर्हितास्त्वां प्रतिपालयन्ति; काष्ठां प्रपद्यन्तमुदक्पतङ्गम् ||१५||

व्यावृत्तमात्रे भगवत्युदीचीं; सूर्ये दिशं कालवशात्प्रपन्ने |
गन्तासि लोकान्पुरुषप्रवीर; नावर्तते यानुपलभ्य विद्वान् ||१६||

अमुं च लोकं त्वयि भीष्म याते; ज्ञानानि नङ्क्ष्यन्त्यखिलेन वीर |
अतः स्म सर्वे त्वयि सन्निकर्षं; समागता धर्मविवेचनाय ||१७||

तज्ज्ञातिशोकोपहतश्रुताय; सत्याभिसन्धाय युधिष्ठिराय |
प्रब्रूहि धर्मार्थसमाधियुक्त् मर्थ्यं वचोऽस्यापनुदास्य शोकम् ||१८||

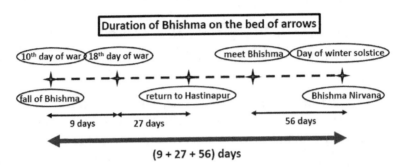

This narration of Bhishma-nirvana, from the Mahabharata text, conclusively proves the duration of Bhishma on the bed of arrows to be that of at least 92 days.

This duration of a minimum interval of 92 days, between the 10th day of the war and the day of winter solstice, is of great importance in determining the chronology of the Mahabharata war. However, before we do that, we must state additional evidence. There is additional evidence that further corroborates the statement of Krishna when he told Bhishma that there were an additional 56 days before Bhishma was going to pass away. This evidence allows us to determine the duration of Bhishma-Yudhishthira samvada when Bhishma advised Yudhishthira on aspects of Dharma, Raja-dharma, and Moksha-dharma.

3.2 Bhishma-Yudhishthira Samvada

No researcher of the past has determined the duration of Bhishma-Yudhishthira samvada, when Bhishma advised Yudhishthira on various aspects of Raja-dharma and Moksha-dharma.

Late Shri Gopal Nilkanth Dandekar (lovingly "Gonida" to Marathi readers) was the first to implicitly recognize the total duration of Bhishma on the bed of arrows as being greater than 92 days. It is worth recognizing that he was writing a summary of entire Mahabharata narration and was not at all focused on either determining or explaining chronology of Mahabharata events. I deliberately point out these findings of "Gonida" to illustrate that what was missed (or deliberately ignored) by Mahabharata researchers dedicated to chronology of Mahabharata events was casually identified by a writer focused on purely Mahabharata narration with no concern for chronology.

We can estimate this duration to be equal to 6 days when Yudhishthira visited Bhishma every day from Hastinapura, listened to Bhishma's advice, and then returned to Hastinapura at the end of the day. At the end of the sixth day, Bhishma asked Yudhishthira to go back to Hastinapura and not return until the sun had turned north, i.e., the day afer the day of winter solstice. Upon this advice of Bhishma, Yudhishthira went back to Hastinapura, stayed there, and only returned to Bhishma at Kurukshetra when the sun turned north.

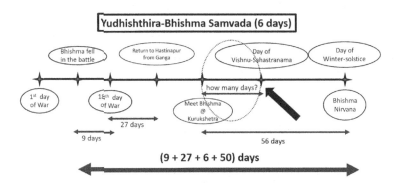

3.2.1 56th Day Before Bhishma-nirvana

As Yudhishthira, his brothers, Krishna and Satyaki, Sanjaya, Yuyutsu and Kripacharya, spent time in the company of sages and Bhishma, the sun turned towards the western horizon and sages asked permission to leave saying that they will return the next day. Yudhishthira and his party also asked permission of Bhishma to leave and boarded their chariots. The entourage of Yudhishthira, with its chariots, horses, and his soilders looked like an east-west

flowing river river Narmada. As they marched towards Hastinapura, the moon rose in the sky and delighted everyone. They
entered Hastinpura, exhausted.

Shanti (CE 52:26-34, GP 52:26-34)

ततो मुहूर्तादद्भगवान्सहस्रांशुर्दिवाकरः |
दहन्वनमिवैकान्ते प्रतीच्यां प्रत्यदृश्यत ||२६||

ततो महर्षयः सर्वे समुत्थाय जनार्दनम् |
भीष्ममामान्त्रयां चक्रू राजानं च युधिष्ठिरम् ||२७||

ततः प्रणाममकरोत्केशवः पाण्डवस्तथा |
सात्यकिः सञ्जयश्चैव स च शारद्वतः कृपः ||२८||

ततस्ते धर्मनिरताः सम्यक्तैरभिपूजिताः |
श्वः समेष्याम इत्युक्त्वा यथेष्टं त्वरिता ययुः ||२९||

तथैवामन्त्र्य गाङ्गेयं केशवस्ते च पाण्डवाः |
प्रदक्षिणमुपावृत्य रथानारुरुहुः शुभान् ||३०||

ततो रथैः काञ्चनदन्तकूबरैः; महीधराभैः समदैश्च दन्तिभिः |
हयैः सुपर्णैरिव चाशुगामिभिः; पदातिभिश्चात्तशरासनादिभिः ||३१||

ययौ रथानां पुरतो हि सा चमूः स्तथैव पश्चादतिमात्रसारिणी |
पुरश्च पश्चाच्च यथा महानदी; पुरक्षवन्तं गिरिमेत्य नर्मदा ||३२||

ततः पुरस्तादद्भगवान्निशाकरः; समुत्थितस्तामभिहर्षयंश्चमूम् |
दिवाकरापीतरसास्तथौषधीः; पुनः स्वकेनैव गुणेन योजयन् ||३३||

ततः पुरं सुरपुरसंनिभद्युति प्रविश्य ते यदुवृषपाण्डवास्तदा |
यथोचितान्भवनवरान्समाविश; ज्श्रमान्विता मृगपतयो गुहा इव ||३४||

3.2.2. 55ᵗʰ Day Before Bhishma-nirvana

Krishna slept on a comfortable bed and woke up early morning to complete his morning-prayers.

Shanti (CE 53:1-2, GP 53:1-2)

ततः प्रविश्य भवनं प्रसुप्तो मधुसूदनः |
याममात्रावशेषायां यामिन्यां प्रत्यबुध्यत ||१||

स ध्यानपथमाश्रित्य सर्वज्ञानानि माधवः |
अवलोक्य ततः पश्चाद्दध्यौ ब्रह्म सनातनम् ||२||

When Krishna has completed his "Pratah-karma," he asked Satyaki to check if Yudhishthira was ready. Satyaki conveyed the message to Yudhishthira, and Yudhishthira asked Arjuna to have chariots ready and informed him of his decision to visit Bhishma without the entourage of soldiers to avoid inconvenience and disturbance to Bhishma. Yudhishthira also expressed his wish to avoid company of numerous others while visiting Bhishma by stating that Bhishma would be advising and counseling him on deeper secrets of Raja-dharma and thus better to avoid presence of common folks.

Shanti (CE 53:10-16, GP 53: 10-16)

गच्छ शैनेय जानीहि गत्वा राजनिवेशनम् |
अपि सज्जो महातेजा भीष्मं द्रष्टुं युधिष्ठिरः ||१०||

ततः कृष्णस्य वचनात्सात्यकिस्त्वरितो ययौ |

उपगम्य च राजानं युधिष्ठिरमुवाच ह ||११||

युक्तो रथवरो राजन्वासुदेवस्य धीमतः |
समीपमापगेयस्य प्रयास्यति जनार्दनः ||१२||

भवत्प्रतीक्षः कृष्णोऽसौ धर्मराज महाद्युते |
यदत्रानन्तरं कृत्यं तदभवान्कर्तुमर्हति ||१३||

युधिष्ठिर उवाच||
युज्यतां मे रथवरः फल्गुनाप्रतिमद्युते |
न सैनिकैश्च यातव्यं यास्यामो वयमेव हि ||१४||
न च पीडयितव्यो मे भीष्मो धर्मभृतां वरः |
अतः पुरःसराश्चापि निवर्तन्तु धनञ्जय ||१५||

अद्यप्रभृति गाङ्गेयः परं गुह्यं प्रवक्ष्यति |
ततो नेच्छामि कौन्तेय पृथग्जनसमागमम् ||१६||

Yudhishthir, along with his brothers, Krishna, and Satyaki left for Kurukshetra and soon arrived near Bhishma, who was surrounded by sages.

Shanti (CE 53:17-27, GP 53: 17-28)

वैशम्पायन उवाच||
तद्वाक्यमाकर्ण्य तथा कुन्तीपुत्रो धनञ्जयः |
युक्तं रथवरं तस्मा आचचक्षे नरर्षभ ||१७||

ततो युधिष्ठिरो राजा यमौ भीमार्जुनावपि |
भूतानीव समस्तानि ययुः कृष्णनिवेशनम् ||१८||

आगच्छत्स्वथ कृष्णोऽपि पाण्डवेषु महात्मसु |
शैनेयसहितो धीमान्नथमेवान्वपद्यत ||१९||

रथस्थाः संविदं कृत्वा सुखां पृष्ट्वा च शर्वरीम् |
मेघघोषै रथवरैः प्रययुस्ते महारथाः ||२०||

मेघपुष्पं बलाहं च सैन्यं सुग्रीवमेव च |
दारुकश्चोदयामास वासुदेवस्य वाजिनः ||२१||

ते हया वासुदेवस्य दारुकेण प्रचोदिताः |
गां खुराग्रैस्तथा राजँल्लिखन्तः प्रययुस्तदा ||२२||

ते ग्रसन्त इवाकाशं वेगवन्तो महाबलाः |
क्षेत्रं धर्मस्य कृत्स्नस्य कुरुक्षेत्रमवातरन् ||२३||

ततो ययुर्यत्र भीष्मः शरतल्पगतः प्रभुः |
आस्ते ब्रह्मर्षिभिः सार्धं ब्रह्मा देवगणैर्यथा ||२४||

ततोऽवतीर्य गोविन्दो रथात्स च युधिष्ठिरः |
भीमो गाण्डीवधन्वा च यमौ सात्यकिरेव च ||२५||
ऋषीनभ्यर्चयामासुः करानुद्यम्य दक्षिणान् ||२५||

स तैः परिवृतो राजा नक्षत्रैरिव चन्द्रमाः |
अभ्याजगाम गाङ्गेयं ब्रह्माणमिव वासवः ||२६||

शरतल्पे शयानं तमादित्यं पतितं यथा |
ददर्श स महाबाहुर्भयादागतसाध्वसः ||२७||

Bhishma began responding to queries of Yudhishthira and instructed Yudhishthira on Raja-dharma.

When Yudhishthira noticed that the sun had moved towards the western horizon, he asked Bhishma for permission to leave. On the way to Hastinpura, they bathed in the Drishtavati river, conducted their Dhyana and Japa, and then reached Hastinapura.

Shanti (CE 58:27-30, GP 58:27-30)

ततो दीनमना भीष्ममुवाच कुरुसत्तमः |
नेत्राभ्यामश्रुपूर्णाभ्यां पादौ तस्य शनैः स्पृशन् ||२७||

श्व इदानीं स्वसंदेहं प्रक्ष्यामि त्वं पितामह |
उपैति सविताप्यस्तं रसमापीय पार्थिवम् ||२८||

ततो द्विजातीनभिवाद्य केशवः; कृपश्च ते चैव युधिष्ठिरादयः |
प्रदक्षिणीकृत्य महानदीसुतं; ततो रथानारुरुहुर्मुदा युताः ||२९||

दृषद्वतीं चाप्यवगाह्य सुव्रताः; कृतोदकार्याः कृतजप्यमङ्गलाः |
उपास्य सन्ध्यां विधिवत्परन्तपा; स्ततः पुरं ते विविशुर्गजाह्वयम् ||३०||

3.2.3. 54th Day Before Bhishma-nirvana

The next day, the Pandava brothers along with Krishna and Satyaki left for Kurukshetra and arrived near Bhishma.

Shanti (CE 59:1-3, GP 59:1-3)

ततः काल्यं समुत्थाय कृतपौर्वाह्णिकक्रियाः |
ययुस्ते नगराकारै रथैः पाण्डवयादवाः ||१||

प्रपद्य च कुरुक्षेत्रं भीष्ममासाद्य चानघम् ।
सुखां च रजनीं पृष्ट्वा गाङ्गेयं रथिनां वरम् ॥२॥

व्यासादीनभिवाद्यर्षीन्सर्वैस्तैश्चाभिनन्दिताः ।
निषेदुरभितो भीष्मं परिवार्य समन्ततः ॥३॥

After a long discussion that covered multiple subjects, the Mahabharata narration, thankfully, informs us that Yudhishthira and the party left for Hastinapura, where Yudhishthira continued his discussion with his brothers. We would estimate this as the end of day 54.

Shanti (CE 161:1, GP 167:1)

इत्युक्तवति भीष्मे तु तूष्णीम्भूते युधिष्ठिरः ।
पप्रच्छावसरं गत्वा भ्रातृन्विदुरपञ्चमान् ॥१॥

Yudhishthira had a long discussion with his brothers. He praised them at the end of the discussion and then went back to Bhishma to ask further questions. We estimate this as the end of day 54 (before Bhishma-nirvana), i.e., when he held discussions with his brothers in Hastinapura.

Shanti (CE 161:48, GP 167:50-51)

सुचारुवर्णाक्षरशब्दभूषितां, मनोनुगां निर्धुतवाक्यकण्टकाम् ।
निशम्य तां पार्थिव पार्थभाषितां, गिरं नरेन्द्राः प्रशंसुरेव ते ॥४८॥
पुनश्च पप्रच्छ सरिद्वरासुतं, ततः परं धर्ममहीनसत्त्वः ॥४८॥

3.2.4 53rd Day Before Bhishma-nirvana

Yudhishthira went back to Bhishma and began asking him questions.

45

Shanti (CE 162:1, GP 168:1)

पितामह महाप्राज्ञ कुरूणां कीर्तिवर्धन |
प्रश्नं कञ्चित्प्रवक्ष्यामि तन्मे व्याख्यातुमर्हसि ||१||

We do not have specific descriptions of Yudhishthira and his brothers returning to Hastinapura at the end of the 53rd day before Bhishma-nirvana.

3.2.5 52nd Day Before Bhishma-nirvana

We do not have descriptions of the arrival at Kurukshetra or the departure for Hastinapura by Yudhishthira and his party for the 52nd day before Bhishma-nirvana. However, we have conclusive evidence for its existence due to other chronology narrations.

3.2.6 51st Day Before Bhishma-nirvana

Yudhishthir went back to Bhishma and began asking questions.

Anushasan (GP 110:1)

शरतल्पगतं भीष्मं वृद्धं कुरुपितामहम् |
उपगम्य महाप्राज्ञः पर्यपृच्छद्युधिष्ठिरः||१||

We do know that these descriptions refer to Yudhishthir's arrival at Kurukshetra, on the 51st day before Bhishma-nirvana because he was accompanied by Dhritarashtra.

Anushasan (CE 112:6-7, GP 111.6-7)

तयोः संवदतोरेवं पार्थगाङ्गेययोस्तदा |
आजगाम विशुद्धात्मा भगवान्स बृहस्पतिः ||६||

ततो राजा समुत्थाय धृतराष्ट्रपुरोगमः |
पूजामनुपमां चक्रे सर्वे ते च सभासदः ||७||

On this day, Bhishma recited one-thousand names in praise of Krishna, which is now known as "Vishnu-sahasra-naama."

Bhishma continued explaining and responding to other questions of Yudhishthira and then became silent. When Vyasa noticed that Bhishma had become silent, he turned to Bhishma and told him that Yudhishthira had returned to his normal state and that Bhishma should give permission to Yudhishthira, his brothers, Krishna, and others to return to Hastinapura.

Anushasan (CE 152:1-3, GP 166:4-7)

तूष्णीम्भूते तदा भीष्मे पटे चित्रमिवार्पितम् |
मुहूर्तमिव च ध्यात्वा व्यासः सत्यवतीसुतः||१||
नृपं शयानं गाङ्गेयमिदमाह वचस्तदा ||१||

राजन्प्रकृतिमापन्नः कुरुराजो युधिष्ठिरः |
सहितो भ्रातृभिः सर्वैः पार्थिवैश्चानुयायिभिः ||२||

उपास्ते त्वां नरव्याघ्र सह कृष्णेन धीमता |
तमिमं पुरयानाय त्वमनुज्ञातुमर्हसि ||३||

Bhishma made his parting remarks to Yudhishthira and specifically asked Yudhishthira to return only when the sun turned north.

Anushasan (CE 152:10, GP 166:14)

आगन्तव्यं च भवता समये मम पार्थिव |
विनिवृत्ते दिनकरे प्रवृत्ते चोत्तरायणे ||१०||

Yudhishthira agreed to the instructions of Bhishma, paid his obeisances, and then left for Hastinapura. He soon entered Hastinapura in the company of his brothers, Krishna, Dhritarashtra, Gandhari, sages, his ministers, and citizens of his kingdom.

Anushasan (CE 152:11-13, GP 166:15-17)

तथेत्युक्त्वा तु कौन्तेयः सोऽभिवाद्य पितामहम् |
प्रययौ सपरीवारो नगरं नागसाह्वयम् ||११||

धृतराष्ट्रं पुरस्कृत्य गान्धारीं च पतिव्रताम् |
सह तैरृषिभिः सर्वैर्भातृभिः केशवेन च ||१२||

पौरजानपदैश्चैव मन्त्रिवृद्धैश्च पार्थिवः |
प्रविवेश कुरुश्रेष्ठ पुरं वारणसाह्वयम् ||१३||

This was the end of the six-day-long Bhishma-Yudhishthira samvada.

3.3 The Day of Bhishma-nirvana

Upon his return to Hastinapura, Yudhishthira honored the citizens of Hastinapura and his kingdom and then asked them to return to their homes. He compensated with distribution of wealth, women of his kingdom, who had lost either their husbands or children.

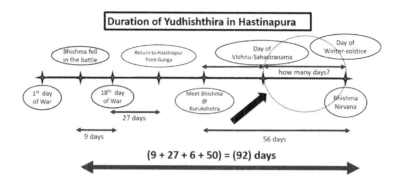

Anushasan (CE 153:1-2, GP 167:1-2)

ततः कुन्तीसुतो राजा पौरजानपदं जनम् |
पूजयित्वा यथान्यायमनुजज्ञे गृहान्प्रति ||१||

सान्त्वयामास नारीश्च हतवीरा हतेश्वराः |
विपुलैरर्थदानैश्च तदा पाण्डुसुतो नृपः ||२||

Yudhishthira spent 50 nights in Hastinapura, and then when the sun turned north, he left Hastinapura with his associates for Kurukshetra to meet Bhishma.

Anushasan (CE 153:5-6, GP 167:5-6)

उषित्वा शर्वरीः श्रीमान्पञ्चाशन्नगरोत्तमे |
समयं कौरवाग्र्यस्य सस्मार पुरुषर्षभः ||५||

स निर्ययौ गजपुराद्याजकैः परिवारितः |
दृष्ट्वा निवृत्तमादित्यं प्रवृत्तं चोत्तरायणम् ||६||

The fact that Yudhishthira spent 50 nights in Hastinapura allows us to estimate the duration of the Bhishma-Yudhishthira samvada to be equal to 6 days.

The Mahabharata text is silent on the exact duration between the arrival of Yudhishthira from the bank of the Ganga river to Hastinapura and his first meeting with Bhishma at Kurukshetra. Let's make this unknown duration equal to "X" days. We do know, based on the Mahahbarata text, that there was at least one night spent at Hastinapura before Yudhishthira went to see Bhishma. This means the minimum value for $X = 1$.

We can summarize the details for the duration of Bhishma on the bed of arrows:

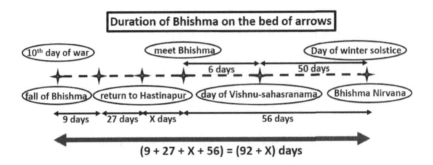

Yudhishthira carried things necessary for Bhishma's "Agni-sanskara" along with him.

Anushasan (CE 153:7-8, GP 167: 7-8)

घृतं माल्यं च गन्धांश्च क्षौमाणि च युधिष्ठिरः |
चन्दनागरुमुख्यानि तथा कालागरूणि च ||७||

प्रस्थाप्य पूर्वं कौन्तेयो भीष्मसंसाधनाय वै |
माल्यानि च महार्हाणि रत्नानि विविधानि च ||८||

Yudhishthira was accompanied by Dhritarashtra, Gandhari, Kunti, Pandava brothers, Krishna, Vidura, Yuyutsu, Satyaki, and others.

Anushasan (CE 153:9-10, GP 167: 9-10)

धृतराष्ट्रं पुरस्कृत्य गान्धारीं च यशस्विनीम् |
मातरं च पृथां धीमान्भ्रातृंश्च पुरुषर्षभः ||९||

जनार्दनेनानुगतो विदुरेण च धीमता |
युयुत्सुना च कौरव्यो युयुधानेन चाभिभो||१०||

The praises were sung for these royal personalities as they arrived near Bhishma at Kurukshetra. Various sages including Vyasa, Narada, Asita, Deval, and others were sitting next to Bhishma. Warriors who had arrived from various places and who survived through the Mahabharata war were protecting Bhishma from all sides. Yudhishthira got down from the chariot, along with his brothers, approached Bhishma, paid his obeisances and told Bhishma that he had arrived at the right time, along with Dhritarashtra, Krishna, as well as citizens of the Kuru kingdom.

Anushasan (CE 153:11-22, GP 167: 11-22)

महता राजभोग्येन परिबर्हेण संवृतः |
स्तूयमानो महाराज भीष्मस्याग्नीननुव्रजन् ||११||

निश्चक्राम पुरातस्मादयथा देवपतिस्तथा |
आससाद कुरुक्षेत्रे ततः शान्तनवं नृपम् ||१२||

उपास्यमानं व्यासेन पाराशर्येण धीमता |
नारदेन च राजर्षे देवलेनासितेन च ||१३||

हतशिष्टैर्नृपैश्चान्यैर्नानादेशसमागतैः |
रक्षिभिश्च महात्मानं रक्ष्यमाणं समन्ततः ||१४||

51

शयानं वीरशयने ददर्श नृपतिस्ततः |
ततो रथादवारोहद्भ्रातृभिः सह धर्मराट् ||१५||

अभिवाद्याथ कौन्तेयः पितामहमरिंदमम् |
द्वैपायनादीन्विप्रांश्च तैश्च प्रत्यभिनन्दितः ||१६||

ऋत्विग्भिर्ब्रह्मकल्पैश्च भ्रातृभिश्च सहाच्युतः |
आसाद्य शरतल्पस्थमृषिभिः परिवारितम् ||१७||

अब्रवीद्भरतश्रेष्ठं धर्मराजो युधिष्ठिरः |
भ्रातृभिः सह कौरव्य शयानं निम्नगासुतम् ||१८||

युधिष्ठिरोऽहं नृपते नमस्ते जाह्नवीसुत |
शृणोषि चेन्महाबाहो ब्रूहि किं करवाणि ते ||१९||

प्राप्तोऽस्मि समये राजन्नग्नीनादाय ते विभो |
आचार्या ब्राह्मणाश्चैव ऋत्विजो भ्रातरश्च मे ||२०||

पुत्रश्च ते महातेजा धृतराष्ट्रो जनेश्वरः |
उपस्थितः सहामात्यो वासुदेवश्च वीर्यवान् ||२१||

हतशिष्टाश्च राजानः सर्वे च कुरुजाङ्गलाः |
तान्पश्य कुरुशार्दूल समुन्मीलय लोचने ||२२||

Bhishma opened his eyes and noticed everyone who was sur-
rounding him and then held hands of Yudhishthira.

Anushasan (CE 153:24-25, GP 167:24-25)

एवमुक्तस्तु गाङ्गेयः कुन्तीपुत्रेण धीमता |
ददर्श भारतान्सर्वान्स्थितान्सम्परिवार्य तम् ||२४||

ततश्चलवलिर्भीष्मः प्रगृह्य विपुलं भुजम् |
ओघमेघस्वनो वाग्मी काले वचनमब्रवीत् ||२५||

Bhishma told Yudhishthira that it was indeed fortunate that Yudhishtira had arrived along with his ministers, and that the sun had turned to the north.

Anushasan (CE 153:26, GP 167:26)

दिष्ट्या प्राप्तोऽसि कौन्तेय सहामात्यो युधिष्ठिर |
परिवृत्तो हि भगवान्सहस्रांशुर्दिवाकरः ||२६||

What Bhishma said next is rather trivial for establishing or contradicting the total duration of Bhishma lying on the bed of arrows. On the other hand, these two verses of the Mahabharata text have confused all Mahabharata researchers. These two verses and their confused interpretation coupled with utter ignorance about the logic of scientific method, on the part of Mahabharata researchers, has created enormous confusion regarding the chronology of the Mahabharata war. We will return to these two verses, analyze their details and analyze illogical works of numerous Mahabharata researchers in chapter 10 – "Conflicting Observations."

Bhishma told Yudhishthira that the period of the <u>past</u> 58 nights of lying on the bed of arrows was tiresome, and Bhishma felt it as if he was lying there for 100 years. Bhishma further stated that it appeared to him that it was the lunar month of Magha and that either the 1/3 (<u>or 1/4</u>) of Paksha (<u>or month</u>) had elapsed (<u>or remaining</u>).

Anushasan (CE 153:27-28, GP 167: 27-28)

अष्टपञ्चाशतं रात्र्यः शयानस्याद्य मे गताः |
शरेषु निशिताग्रेषु यथा वर्षशतं तथा ||२७||

माघोऽयं समनुप्राप्तो मासः पुण्यो युधिष्ठिर |
त्रिभागशेषः पक्षोऽयं शुक्लो भवितुमर्हति ||२८||

Bhishma then called Dhritarashtra near him and asked him to give up all sadness and to treat the Pandavas as his own. Bhishma then asked Krishna for his permission for Bhishma to leave his body. Then turning to Yudhishthira, he said his parting words and became silent.

Anushasan (CE 153:29-50, GP 167:29-52)

एवमुक्त्वा तु गाङ्गेयो धर्मपुत्रं युधिष्ठिरम् |
धृतराष्ट्रमथामन्त्र्य काले वचनमब्रवीत् ||२९||

राजन्निदितधर्मोऽसि सुनिर्णीतार्थसंशयः |
बहुश्रुता हि ते विप्रा बहवः पर्युपासिताः ||३०||

वेदशास्त्राणि सर्वाणि धर्माश्च मनुजेश्वर |
वेदांश्च चतुरः साङ्गान्निखिलेनावबुध्यसे ||३१||

न शोचितव्यं कौरव्य भवितव्यं हि तत्तथा |
श्रुतं देवरहस्यं ते कृष्णद्वैपायनादपि ||३२||

यथा पाण्डोः सुता राजंस्तथैव तव धर्मतः |
तान्पालय स्थितो धर्मे गुरुशुश्रूषणे रतान् ||३३||

धर्मराजो हि शुद्धात्मा निदेशे स्थास्यते तव |
आनृशंस्यपरं ह्येनं जानामि गुरुवत्सलम् ||३४||

तव पुत्रा दुरात्मानः क्रोधलोभपरायणाः |
ईर्ष्याभिभूता दुर्वृत्तास्तान्न शोचितुमर्हसि ||३५||

वैशम्पायन उवाच||
एतावदुक्त्वा वचनं धृतराष्ट्रं मनीषिणम् |
वासुदेवं महाबाहुमभ्यभाषत कौरवः ||३६||

भगवन्देवदेवेश सुरासुरनमस्कृत |
त्रिविक्रम नमस्तेऽस्तु शङ्खचक्रगदाधर ||३७||

अनुजानीहि मां कृष्ण वैकुण्ठ पुरुषोत्तम |
रक्ष्याश्च ते पाण्डवेया भवान्ह्येषां परायणम् ||३८||

उक्तवानस्मि दुर्बुद्धिं मन्दं दुर्योधनं पुरा |
यतः कृष्णस्ततो धर्मो यतो धर्मस्ततो जयः ||३९||

वासुदेवेन तीर्थेन पुत्र संशाम्य पाण्डवैः |
सन्धानस्य परः कालस्तवेति च पुनः पुनः ||४०||

न च मे तद्वचो मूढः कृतवान्स सुमन्दधीः |
घातयित्वेह पृथिवीं ततः स निधनं गतः ||४१||

त्वां च जानाम्यहं वीर पुराणमृषिसत्तमम् |
नरेण सहितं देवं बदर्यां सुचिरोषितम् ||४२||

तथा मे नारदः प्राह व्यासश्च सुमहातपाः |
नरनारायणावेतौ सम्भूतौ मनुजेष्विति ||४३||

वासुदेव उवाच||

अनुजानामि भीष्म त्वां वसूनाप्नुहि पार्थिव |
न तेऽस्ति वृजिनं किञ्चिन्मया दृष्टं महाद्युते ||४४||

पितृभक्तोऽसि राजर्षे मार्कण्डेय इवापरः |
तेन मृत्युस्तव वशे स्थितो भृत्य इवानतः ||४५||

वैशम्पायन उवाच||

एवमुक्तस्तु गाङ्गेयः पाण्डवानिदमब्रवीत् |
धृतराष्ट्रमुखांश्चापि सर्वान्ससुहृदस्तथा ||४६||

प्राणानुत्स्रष्टुमिच्छामि तन्मानुज्ञातुमर्हथ |
सत्ये प्रयतितव्यं वः सत्यं हि परमं बलम् ||४७||

आनृशंस्यपरैर्भाव्यं सदैव नियतात्मभिः |
ब्रह्मण्यैर्धर्मशीलैश्च तपोनित्यैश्च भारत ||४८||

इत्युक्त्वा सुहृदः सर्वान्सम्परिष्वज्य चैव ह |
पुनरेवाब्रवीद्धीमान्युधिष्ठिरमिदं वचः ||४९||

ब्राह्मणाश्चैव ते नित्यं प्राज्ञाश्चैव विशेषतः |
आचार्या ऋत्विजश्चैव पूजनीया नराधिप ||५०||

Bhishma focused internally and began releasing his "prana" and became one with the universe.

Anushasan (CE 154:1-7, GP 168:1-9)

एवमुक्त्वा कुरून्सर्वान्भीष्मः शान्तनवस्तदा ।
तूष्णीं बभूव कौरव्यः स मुहूर्तमरिंदम ॥१॥

धारयामास चात्मानं धारणासु यथाक्रमम् ।
तस्योर्ध्वमगमन्प्राणाः संनिरुद्धा महात्मनः ॥२॥

इदमाश्चर्यमासीच्च मध्ये तेषां महात्मनाम् ।
यद्यन्मुञ्चति गात्राणां स शन्तनुसुतस्तदा ॥३॥
तत्तद्विशल्यं भवति योगयुक्तस्य तस्य वै ॥३॥

क्षणेन प्रेक्षतां तेषां विशल्यः सोऽभवत्तदा ।
तं दृष्ट्वा विस्मिताः सर्वे वासुदेवपुरोगमाः ॥४॥
सह तैर्मुनिभिः सर्वैस्तदा व्यासादिभिर्नृप ॥४॥

संनिरुद्धस्तु तेनात्मा सर्वेष्वायतनेषु वै ।
जगाम भित्त्वा मूर्धानं दिवमभ्युत्पपात च ॥५॥

महोल्केव च भीष्मस्य मूर्धदेशाज्जनाधिप ।
निःसृत्याकाशमाविश्य क्षणेनान्तरधीयत ॥६॥

एवं स नृपशार्दूल नृपः शान्तनवस्तदा ।
समयुज्यत लोकैः स्वैर्भरतानां कुलोद्वहः ॥७॥

Vidura, Yuyutsu, and the Pandava brothers created a pyre using wood and perfumes while the rest of the crowd watched. Yudhishthira and Vidura covered Bhishma with flower garlands, a silk cloth, and placed his body on the pyre.

Anushasan (CE 154:8-9, GP 168:10-12)

ततस्त्वादाय दारूणि गन्धांश्च विविधान्बहून् |
चितां चक्रुर्महात्मानः पाण्डवा विदुरस्तथा ||८||
युयुत्सुश्चापि कौरव्यः प्रेक्षकास्त्वितरेऽभवन् ||८||

युधिष्ठिरस्तु गाङ्गेयं विदुरश्च महामतिः |
छादयामासतुरुभौ क्षौमैर्माल्यैश्च कौरवम् ||९||

The Pandava brothers and the Kuru women also participated in various ways. The Pandavas performed "Pitru-medha" and offered many oblations to the "Agni," and while "Sama-gana" continued, Dhritarashtra lit the pyre. All present did "Parikrama" around Bhishma.

Anushasan (CE 154:10-14, GP 168:13-17)

धारयामास तस्याथ युयुत्सुश्छत्रमुत्तमम् |
चामरव्यजने शुभ्रे भीमसेनार्जुनावुभौ ||१०||
उष्णीषे पर्यगृह्णीतां माद्रीपुत्रावुभौ तदा ||१०||

स्त्रियः कौरवनाथस्य भीष्मं कुरुकुलोद्भवम् |
तालवृन्तान्युपादाय पर्यवीजन्समन्ततः ||११||

ततोऽस्य विधिवच्चक्रुः पितृमेधं महात्मनः |
याजका जुहुवुश्चाग्निं जगुः सामानि सामगाः ||१२||

ततश्चन्दनकाष्ठैश्च तथा कालेयकैरपि |
कालागरुप्रभृतिभिर्गन्धैश्चोच्चावचैस्तथा ||१३||

समवच्छाद्य गाङ्गेयं प्रज्वाल्य च हुताशनम् |
अपसव्यमकुर्वन्त धृतराष्ट्रमुखा नृपाः ||१४||

After this, they all went to the bank of the river Ganga and did "Jala-kriya" for Bhishma and then returned to Hastinapura.

Anushasan (CE 154:15-17, GP 168:18-20)

संस्कृत्य च कुरुश्रेष्ठं गाङ्गेयं कुरुसत्तमाः |
जग्मुर्भागीरथीतीरमृषिजुष्टं कुरूद्वहाः ||१५||

अनुगम्यमाना व्यासेन नारदेनासितेन च |
कृष्णेन भरतस्त्रीभिर्ये च पौराः समागताः ||१६||

उदकं चक्रिरे चैव गाङ्गेयस्य महात्मनः |
विधिवत्क्षत्रियश्रेष्ठाः स च सर्वो जनस्तदा ||१७||

Summary

A crisp and clear timeline for the events of Bhishma-nirvana can be gleaned from the Mahabharata text.

(1) Bhishma was on the bed of arrows for more than 92 days. We will use 92 as a lower limit in estimating the constraints related to events of Bhishma-nirvana.
(2) Bhishma fell in the battle on the 10th day of the war and since then was on the bed of arrows until the day of the winter solstice. The war continued for an additional eight days.
(3) Yudhishthira and his party spent a month-long interval on the bank of the river Ganga r after the war was over and before returning to Hastinapura.

(4) In Hastinapura, Yudhisthira was coronated as the King and then went to meet Bhishma. It is on this day that Krishna told Bhishma that Bhishma had 56 more days to live.

(5) Yudhisthira visited Bhishma every day for six consecutive days during which Bhishma advised him on various subjects of Raja-dharma and Moksha-dharma. Bhishma recited "Vishnu-Sahasra-naama" to all present on the sixth and the last day and then asked Yudhishtira to return to Hastinapura, and only come back to him when the sun turned north. (i.e., after the day of the winter solstice).

(6) Yudhishthira returned to Hastinapura and stayed there for 50 nights before returning to Bhishma. Bhishma passed away on that day.

Astronomy Evidence

"It's been said that astronomy is a humbling and, I might add, a character-building experience."
- Carl Sagan

The chronology evidence of the Mahabharata text decisively proves that the minimum duration of Bhishma on the bed of arrows must equal 92 days. This is an extremely robust estimate for the minimum duration of Bhishma on the bed of arrows.

In this chapter, we will analyze evidence of the Mahabharata text to determine the lunar tithi, lunar paksha (fortnight), and lunar month for the day of Bhishma-nirvana. We will also look for any clues that allow us to identify specific lunar month(s) for the timing of the Mahabharata war and for the day of Bhishma-nirvana.

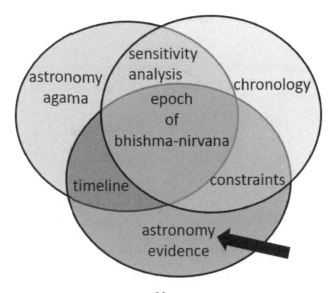

Astronomy evidence can be classified into three segments:

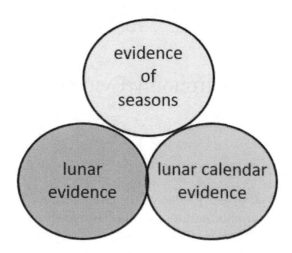

1. Evidence of seasons
2. Lunar evidence
3. Lunar calendar evidence

We will begin with evidence of seasons.

4.1 Evidence of Seasons

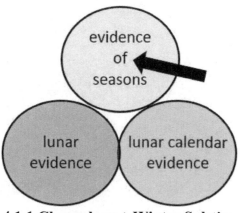

4.1.1 Chronology + Winter Solstice

Bhishma was on the bed of arrows for more than 92 days. Let's use this limiting case of 92 days and go backwards in time from the day of the winter solstice, since the winter solstice was the day of Bhishma-nirvana.

When we go backwards, beginning with the day of the winter solstice, by 60 days, the season of Hemanta would be over. When we go backwards, by an additional 30 days, the second month of Sharad season would be over. We would have to go backwards, for at least two days (total of 92 days), as a limiting case, to the day of the fall of Bhishma in the battle on the 10th day of war. This also means that the Mahabharata war began at least 12 days before the first month of Sharad season was over.

This conclusively establishes that the major part of the Maha-bharata war (minimum of 12 days out of total of 18 days) took place during the first half (first of the 2 months of Sharad season) of the Sharad season.

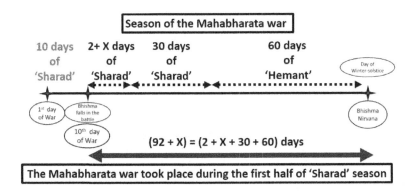

4.1.2 Suitable Season for the War

The Mahabharata text provides additional evidence in support of this conclusion of the war taking place during the first half of Sharad season.

Bhishma refers to lunar months of Margashirsha and Chaitra as times of the year when the crops are matured and water in amply supply, and thus, a good time to initiate military excursions or wars, if the army is ready, since the weather near these lunar months is neither too hot nor too cold.

Shanti (CE 101:8-10, GP 100:10-11)

अभिनीतानि शस्त्राणि योधाश्च कृतनिश्रमाः ||८||

चैत्र्यां वा मार्गशीर्ष्यां वा सेनायोगः प्रशस्यते |
पक्वसस्या हि पृथिवी भवत्यम्बुमती तथा ||९||

नैवातिशीतो नात्युष्णः कालो भवति भारत |
तस्मात्तदा योजयेत परेषां व्यसनेषु वा ||१०||
एतेषु योगाः सेनायाः प्रशस्ताः परबाधने ||१०||

And Krishna refers to, during his conversations with Karna, the upcoming and suitable time for the war. He describes the season as neither too hot nor too cold, when vegetation, fruits, and grains are in ample supply, clean water is available, and the land is free from mud and flies.

Udyoga (CE 140:16-17, GP 142:16-17)

ब्रूयाः कर्ण इतो गत्वा द्रोणं शान्तनवं कृपम् |
सौम्योऽयं वर्तते मासः सुप्रापयवसेन्धनः ||१६||

पक्वौषधिवनस्फीतः फलवानल्पमक्षिकः |
निष्पङ्को रसवत्तोयो नात्युष्णशिशिरः सुखः ||१७||

4.1.3 Evidence of "Sharad" Through 18 Days of the War

The war descriptions of the first 10 days of the war have numerous references to Sharad season.

64

Bhishma (CE 17:28, GP 17:28)

तदङ्गपतिना गुप्तं कृपेण च महात्मना |
शारदाभ्रचयप्रख्यं प्राच्यानामभवद्बलम् ||२८||

Bhishma (CE 55:15, GP 59:16)

विकीर्णैः कवचैश्चित्रैर्ध्वजैश्छत्रैश्च मारिष |
शुशुभे तद्रणस्थानं शरदीव नभस्तलम् ||१५||

Bhishma (CE 89:4, GP 93:4)

अथैनं शरवर्षेण समन्तात्पर्यवारयन् |
पर्वतं वारिधाराभिः शरदीव बलाहकाः ||४||

Bhishma (CE 89:6, GP 93:6)

व्यनदत्सुमहानादं जीमूत इव शारदः |
दिशः खं प्रदिशश्चैव नादयन्भैरवस्वनः ||६||

Bhishma (CE 90:16, GP 94:17)

भूयश्चैनं महाबाहुः शरैः शीघ्रमवाकिरत् |
पर्वतं वारिधाराभिः शरदीव बलाहकः ||१६||

Bhishma (CE 93:22, GP 97:22)

अरजोम्बरसंवीतः सिंहखेलगतिर्नृपः |
शुशुभे विमलार्चिष्मञ्शरदीव दिवाकरः ||२२||

Bhishma (CE 112:130, GP 117:56)

तद्गजाश्वरथौघानां रुधिरेण समुक्षितम् |
छन्नमायोधनं रेजे रक्ताभ्रमिव शारदम् ||१३०||

The descriptions of Sharad season continue through the 5 days of the war when Drona was the leader of Duryodhana's army.

Drona (CE 19:41, GP 20:40)

विक्षरद्भिर्ननदद्भिश्च निपतद्भिश्च वारणैः |
सम्बभूव मही कीर्णा मेघैर्द्यौरिव शारदी ||४१||

Drona (CE 37:20, GP 38:21)

मृदुर्भूत्वा महाराज दारुणः समपद्यत |
वर्षाभ्यतीतो भगवाञ्शरदीव दिवाकरः ||२०||

Drona (CE 96:5, GP 120:5)

सधनुर्मण्डलः सङ्ख्ये तेजोभास्वररश्मिवान् |
शरदीवोदितः सूर्यो नृसूर्यो विरराज ह ||५||

Drona (CE 107:35, GP 132:39)

ताभ्यां मुक्ता व्यकाशन्त कङ्कबर्हिणवाससः |
पङ्क्तयः शरदि मत्तानां सारसानामिवाम्बरे ||३५||

Drona (CE 114:20, GP 139:26)

ततः क्रुद्धः शरानस्यन्सूतपुत्रो व्यरोचत |
मध्यंदिनगतोऽर्चिष्मान्शरदीव दिवाकरः ||२०||

Drona (CE 117:16, GP 142:16-17)

किं मृषोक्तेन बहुना कर्मणा तु समाचर |
शारदस्येव मेघस्य गर्जितं निष्फलं हि ते ||१६||

Drona (CE 155:26, GP 180:26-27)

मध्यङ्गत इवादित्यो यो न शक्यो निरीक्षितुम् |
त्वदीयैः पुरुषव्याघ्र योधमुख्यैर्महात्मभिः ||२६||
शरजालसहस्रांशुः शरदीव दिवाकरः ||२६||

Drona (CE 162:37, GP 187:39)

ते रथान्सूर्यसङ्काशानास्थिताः पुरुषर्षभाः |
अशोभन्त यथा मेघाः शारदाः समुपस्थिताः ||३७||

The descriptions of Sharad season continue through the 2 days of the war when Karna was the leader of Duryodhana's army.

Karna (CE 8:23, GP 12:23)

तस्यायसं वर्मवरं वररत्नविभूषितम् |
तारोद्भासस्य नभसः शारदस्य समत्विषम् ||२३||

Karna (GP 19:51)

तारागणविचित्रस्य निर्मलेन्दुद्युतित्विषः ||५१||
पश्येमां नभसस्तुल्यां शरन्नक्षत्रमालिनीम् |

Karna (CE 68:24, GP 94:15)

विमुक्तयन्त्रैर्निहतैरयस्मयैः; हतानुषङ्गैर्विनिषङ्गबन्धुरैः |
प्रभग्ननीडैर्मणिहेममण्डितैः; स्तृता मही द्यौरिव शारदैर्घनैः ||२४||

The descriptions of Sharad season continue through the last and 18th day of the war when Shalya was the leader of Duryodhana's army.

Shalya (CE 3:28, GP 4:28)

वायुनेव विधूतानि तवानीकानि सर्वशः |
शरदम्भोदजालानि व्यशीर्यन्त समन्ततः ||२८||

Shalya (CE 32:49, GP 33:55)

मा वृथा गर्ज कौन्तेय शारदाभ्रमिवाजलम् |
दर्शयस्व बलं युद्धे यावत्तेऽद्य विद्यते ||४९||

Shalya (CE 45:49, GP 46:55-56)

सा सेना नैरृती भीमा सघण्टोच्छ्रितकेतना |
सभेरीशङ्खमुरजा सायुधा सपताकिनी ||४९||
शारदी द्यौरिवाभाति ज्योतिर्भिरुपशोभिता ||४९||

Shalya (CE 54:27, GP 55:32-33)

अन्योन्यमभिधावन्तौ मत्ताविव महाद्विपौ ।
वाशितासङ्गमे दृप्तौ शरदीव मदोत्कटौ ॥२७॥

The descriptions of Sharad season continue post-war as the Kuru women arrived at Kurukshetra to identify the bodies of their loved ones.

Stri (CE 19:2, GP 19:2)

गजमध्यगतः शेते विकर्णो मधुसूदन ।
नीलमेघपरिक्षिप्तः शरदीव दिवाकरः ॥२॥

Stri (CE 25:16, GP 25:16)

पाञ्चालराज्ञो विपुलं पुण्डरीकाक्ष पाण्डुरम् ।
आतपत्रं समाभाति शरदीव दिवाकरः ॥१६॥

4.2 Lunar Evidence

Lunar phases and positions of the moon define the days of the lunar month. The Mahabharata text preserves detailed evidence through the 18 days of the war.

We will evaluate phases and positions of the moon through the 18 days of the war and one day after the war. This evidence establishes "Shukla paskha" (waxing fortnight) and "Margashirsha Shukla paksha" as the timing of the Mahabharata war. Further, this evidence also corroborates Kartika Amavasya as the first day of the Mahabharata war.

4.2.1 Phases of the Moon

The moon is conspicuous by its absence in Mahabharata descriptions during the first seven days of the War. One must wait until the eighth day of the War to read descriptions of the war scenes and their comparison with the moon, and one must wait until the twelfth day of the war to read descriptions of the full moon. These full moon descriptions continue from the 12th through the 18th day of the war and even on the day after the war.

While the battle stopped immediately at the sunset on the first five days of the war, it extended for some time after sunset on the sixth day. On the seventh day of the war, Duryodhana asked his warriors to hurry up and intensify the attack as the sun turned on the western horizon. However, the battle stopped at sunset. The battle continued into the night on the eighth and ninth day of the war. On the 10th day, the battle came to a standstill with the falling of Bhishma. The warriors were exhausted, and the battle stopped at sunset, on the 11th and 12th day of the war.

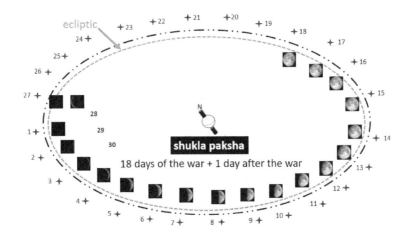

On the 13th day, the Kaurava warriors returned to the camp after killing Abhimanyu while Pandava warriors stood in sadness as the sun set. The fighting continued throughout the night on the 14th day of the war until sunrise, and the fighting continued all day during the 15th day of the war and ended up with the death of Drona. At the end of the 16th day, the darkness set in due to dust, and warriors felt frightened about fighting at night and returned to their camps. Karna was killed at the end of the 17th day, and exhausted Kaurava warriors ran away and were chased by Bhima, Dhrishtadyumna, and other Pandava warriors. Kaurava warriors stayed and slept on the very battlefield during that night. The war ended with the defeat of Duryodhana on the 18th day. However, Duryodhana made Ashwatthama the leader of his army, and Ashwatthama, along with Kripacharya and Kritavarma, attacked the Pandava camp late at night.

These descriptions are consistent with the scenario of war beginning on or near Amavasya day and then continuing for 18 consecutive days, most of it through the Shukla paksha. Let's evaluate this Shukla paksha evidence via the phases of the moon through the 18 days of the war.

71

4.2.1.1 1st Day of the War

The Mahabharata text has many suggestive descriptions of the solar eclipse for the first day of the war. However, there is no clear evidence for the solar eclipse itself.

Bhishma (CE 17:3, GP 17:3)

द्विधाभूत इवादित्य उदये प्रत्यदृश्यत |
ज्वलन्त्या शिखया भूयो भानुमानुदितो दिवि ||३||

Bhishma (CE 19:36-39, GP 37-40)

सन्ध्यां तिष्ठत्सु सैन्येषु सूर्यस्योदयनं प्रति |
प्रावात्सपृष्टतो वायुरनभ्रे स्तनयित्नुमान् ||३६||

विष्वग्वाताश्च वान्त्युग्रा नीचैः शर्करकर्षिणः |
रजश्चोद्धूयमानं तु तमसाच्छादयज्जगत् ||३७||

पपात महती चोल्का प्राङ्मुखी भरतर्षभ |
उद्यन्तं सूर्यमाहत्य व्यशीर्यत महास्वना ||३८||

अथ सज्जीयमानेषु सैन्येषु भरतर्षभ |
निष्प्रभोऽभ्युदियात्सूर्यः सघोषो भूश्चचाल ह ||३९||

Bhishma (CE 42:28, GP 44:28)

उभयोः सेनयोस्तीव्रः सैन्यानां स समागमः |
अन्तर्धीयत चादित्यः सैन्येन रजसावृतः ||२८||

The fighting stopped on the first day with the sunset, and the darkness was such that it was impossible to decipher anything.

Bhishma (CE 45:62, GP 49:52)

ततः सैन्येषु भग्नेषु मथितेषु च सर्वशः |
प्राप्ते चास्तं दिनकरे न प्राज्ञायत किञ्चन ||६२||

4.2.1.2 2nd Day of the War

The fighting stopped on the second day with the sunset.

Bhishma (CE 51:40-43, GP 55:40-43)

एष चास्तं गिरिश्रेष्ठं भानुमान्प्रतिपद्यते |
वपूंषि सर्वलोकस्य संहरन्निव सर्वथा ||४०||

तत्रावहारं सम्प्राप्तं मन्येऽहं पुरुषर्षभ |
श्रान्ता भीताश्च नो योधा न योत्स्यन्ति कथञ्चन ||४१||

एवमुक्त्वा ततो भीष्मो द्रोणमाचार्यसत्तमम् |

अवहारमथो चक्रे तावकानां महारथः ॥४२॥

ततोऽवहारः सैन्यानां तव तेषां च भारत ।
अस्तं गच्छति सूर्येऽभूत्सन्ध्याकाले च वर्तति ॥४३॥

4.2.1.3 3rd Day of the War

Satyaki and Abhimanyu were forced to fight from the same chariot with the Kaurava army on the third day of the war, and the Mahabharata author compares them to the view of the sun and the moon together, as seen on the past/recent (Gatau) Amavasya day.

Bhishma (CE 54:23, GP 58:25)

शुशुभाते तदा तौ तु शैनेयकुरुपुङ्गवौ ।
अमावास्यां गतौ यद्वत्सोमसूर्यौ नभस्तले ॥२३॥

The battlefield on the third day of the war was like the autumnal star-studded sky.

Bhishma (CE 55:15, GP 59:16)

विकीर्णैः कवचैश्चित्रैर्ध्वजैश्छत्रैश्च मारिष ।
शुशुभे तद्रणस्थानं शरदीव नभस्तलम् ॥१५॥

The battle ended with the sunset.

Bhishma (CE 55:127-129, GP 59:131-133)

ततो रविं संहतरश्मिजालं; दृष्ट्वा भृशं शस्त्रपरिक्षताङ्गाः |
तदैन्द्रमस्त्रं विततं सुघोर; मसह्यमुद्वीक्ष्य युगान्तकल्पम् ||१२७||

अथापयानं कुरवः सभीष्माः; सद्रोणदुर्योधनबाह्लिकाश्च |
चक्रुर्निशां सन्धिगतां समीक्ष्य; विभावसोर्लोहितराजियुक्ताम् ||१२८|

अवाप्य कीर्तिं च यशश्च लोके; विजित्य शत्रूंश्च धनञ्जयोऽपि |
ययौ नरेन्द्रैः सह सोदरैश्च; समाप्तकर्मा शिबिरं निशायाम् ||१२९||

4.2.1.4 4th Day of the War

The battle ended with the sunset.

Bhishma (CE 60:73-77, GP 64:81-85)

कौरवास्तु ततो राजन्प्रययुः शिबिरं स्वकम् |
व्रीडमाना निशाकाले पाण्डवेयैः पराजिताः ||७३||

शरविक्षतगात्राश्च पाण्डुपुत्रा महारथाः |
युद्धे सुमनसो भूत्वा शिबिरायैव जग्मिरे ||७४||

पुरस्कृत्य महाराज भीमसेनघटोत्कचौ |
पूजयन्तस्तदान्योन्यं मुदा परमया युताः ||७५||

नदन्तो विविधान्नादांस्तूर्यस्वनविमिश्रितान् ।
सिंहनादांश्च कुर्वाणा विमिश्राञ्शङ्खनिस्वनैः ॥७६॥

विनदन्तो महात्मानः कम्पयन्तश्च मेदिनीम् ।
घट्टयन्तश्च मर्माणि तव पुत्रस्य मारिष ॥७७॥

प्रयाताः शिबिरायैव निशाकाले परन्तपाः ॥७७॥

4.2.1.5 5th Day of the War

The battle ended with the sunset.

Bhishma (CE 70:31-37, GP 74:33-39)

लोहितायति चादित्ये त्वरमाणो धनञ्जयः ।
पञ्चविंशतिसाहस्रान्निजघान महारथान् ॥३१॥

ते हि दुर्योधनादिष्टास्तदा पार्थिनिबर्हणे ।
सम्प्राप्यैव गता नाशं शलभा इव पावकम् ॥३२॥

ततो मत्स्याः केकयाश्च धनुर्वेदविशारदाः ।
परिववुस्तदा पार्थं सहपुत्रं महारथम् ॥३३॥

एतस्मिन्नेव काले तु सूर्योऽस्तमुपगच्छति ।
सर्वेषामेव सैन्यानां प्रमोहः समजायत ॥३४॥

अवहारं ततश्चक्रे पिता देवव्रतस्तव |
सन्ध्याकाले महाराज सैन्यानां श्रान्तवाहनः ||३५||

पाण्डवानां कुरूणां च परस्परसमागमे |
ते सेने भृशसंविग्ने ययतुः स्वं निवेशनम् ||३६||

ततः स्वशिबिरं गत्वा न्यविशंस्तत्र भारत |
पाण्डवाः सृञ्जयैः सार्धं कुरवश्च यथाविधि ||३७||

4.2.1.6 6th Day of the War

Duryodhana made a fresh attack on Bhima as the sun turned red on the western horizon.

Bhishma (CE 75:1, GP 79:1)

ततो दुर्योधनो राजा लोहितायति भास्करे |
सङ्ग्रामरभसो भीमं हन्तुकामोऽभ्यधावत ||१||

The fighting continued for some time after the sunset on the 6th day of the war.

Bhishma (CE 75:55-56, GP 79:60)

अन्योन्यागस्कृतां राजन्यमराष्ट्रविवर्धनम् ||५५||
मुहूर्तास्तमिते सूर्ये चक्रुर्युद्धं सुदारुणम् |
रथिनः सादिनश्चैव व्यकीर्यन्त सहस्रशः ||५६||

Both parties returned to their camps.

Bhishma (CE 75:58-59, GP 79:63-64)

एवं भित्त्वा महेष्वासः पाण्डवानामनीकिनीम् ।
कृत्वावहारं सैन्यानां ययौ स्वशिबिरं नृप ॥५८॥

धर्मराजोऽपि सम्प्रेक्ष्य धृष्टद्युम्नवृकोदरौ ।
मूर्ध्नि चैतावुपाघ्राय संहृष्टः शिबिरं ययौ ॥५९॥

4.2.1.7 7th Day of the War

As the sun turned red on the western horizon, Duryodhana asked warriors of his side to hurry and intensify the attack. The battle ended with the sunset.

Bhishma (CE 82:40-56, GP 86:63-64)

ततो दुर्योधनो राजा लोहितायति भास्करे ।
अब्रवीतावकान्सर्वांस्त्वरध्वमिति भारत ॥४०॥

युध्यतां तु तथा तेषां कुर्वतां कर्म दुष्करम् ।
अस्तं गिरिमथारूढे नप्रकाशति भास्करे ॥४१॥

प्रावर्तत नदी घोरा शोणितौघतरङ्गिणी ।
गोमायुगणसङ्कीर्णा क्षणेन रजनीमुखे ॥४२॥

शिवाभिरशिवाभिश्च रुवद्भिर्भैरवं रवम् |
घोरमायोधनं जज्ञे भूतसङ्घसमाकुलम् ||४३||

राक्षसाश्च पिशाचाश्च तथान्ये पिशिताशनाः |
समन्ततो व्यदृश्यन्त शतशोऽथ सहस्रशः ||४४||

अर्जुनोऽथ सुशर्मादीन्ब्राह्मणस्तान्सपदानुगान् |
विजित्य पृतनामध्ये ययौ स्वशिबिरं प्रति ||४५||

युधिष्ठिरोऽपि कौरव्यो भ्रातृभ्यां सहितस्तदा |
ययौ स्वशिबिरं राजा निशायां सेनया वृतः ||४६||

भीमसेनोऽपि राजेन्द्र दुर्योधनमुखान्रथान् |
अवजित्य ततः सङ्ख्ये ययौ स्वशिबिरं प्रति ||४७||

दुर्योधनोऽपि नृपतिः परिवार्य महारणे |
भीष्मं शान्तनवं तूर्णं प्रयातः शिबिरं प्रति ||४८||

द्रोणो द्रौणिः कृपः शल्यः कृतवर्मा च सात्वतः |
परिवार्य चमूं सर्वां प्रययुः शिबिरं प्रति ||४९||
तथैव सात्यकी राजन्धृष्टद्युम्नश्च पार्षतः |
परिवार्य रणे योधान्ययतुः शिबिरं प्रति ||५०||

एवमेते महाराज तावकाः पाण्डवैः सह |
पर्यवर्तन्त सहिता निशाकाले परन्तपाः ||५१||

ततः स्वशिबिरं गत्वा पाण्डवाः कुरवस्तथा |
न्यविशन्त महाराज पूजयन्तः परस्परम् ||५२||

रक्षां कृत्वात्मनः शूरा न्यस्य गुल्मान्यथाविधि ।
अपनीय च शल्यांस्ते स्नात्वा च विविधैर्जलैः ॥५३॥

कृतस्वस्त्ययनाः सर्वे संस्तूयन्तश्च बन्दिभिः ।
गीतवादित्रशब्देन व्यक्रीडन्त यशस्विनः ॥५४॥

मुहूर्तमिव तत्सर्वमभवत्स्वर्गसंनिभम् ।
न हि युद्धकथां काञ्चित्तत्र चक्रुर्महारथाः ॥५५॥
ते प्रसुप्ते बले तत्र परिश्रान्तजने नृप ।
हस्त्यश्वबहुले राजन्प्रेक्षणीये बभूवतुः ॥५६॥

4.2.1.8 8th Day of the War

As the sunset approached, Ghatotkacha defeated the Kaurava army and warriors of the Kaurava army began running towards their camps. Bhishma and Sanjaya made a feeble attempt to stop them from running away but failed.

Bhishma (CE 90:43-46, GP 94:46-50)

तद्दृष्ट्वा तावकं सैन्यं विद्रुतं शिबिरं प्रति ।
मम प्राक्रोशतो राजंस्तथा देवव्रतस्य च ॥४३॥

युध्यध्वं मा पलायध्वं मायैषा राक्षसी रणे ।
घटोत्कचप्रयुक्तेति नातिष्ठन्त विमोहिताः ॥४४॥
नैव ते श्रद्दधुर्भीता वदतोरावयोर्वचः ॥४४॥

तांश्च प्रद्रवतो दृष्ट्वा जयं प्राप्ताश्च पाण्डवाः |
घटोत्कचेन सहिताः सिंहनादान्प्रचक्रिरे ||४५||
शङ्खदुन्दुभिघोषाश्च समन्तात्सस्वनुभृशम् ||४५||

एवं तव बलं सर्वं हैडिम्बेन दुरात्मना |
सूर्यास्तमनवेलायां प्रभग्नं विद्रुतं दिशः ||४६||

The battle continued into the night and the place looked like the sky filled with planets and nakshatras.

Bhishma (CE 92:73-75, GP 96:75-77)

नरेन्द्रचूडामणिभिर्विचित्रैश्च महाधनैः |
छत्रैस्तथापविद्धैश्च चामरव्यजनैरपि ||७३||

पद्मेन्दुद्युतिभिश्चैव वदनैश्चारुकुण्डलैः |
क्लृप्तश्मश्रुभिरत्यर्थं वीराणां समलङ्कृतैः ||७४||

अपविद्धैर्महाराज सुवर्णोज्ज्वलकुण्डलैः |
ग्रहनक्षत्रशबला द्यौरिवासीद्वसुन्धरा ||७५||

The fight continued into the night on the eighth day of the war until fighters on both sides were utterly exhausted and until leaders of both sides ordered to stop the fight. Many fighters had run away from the battlefield, while many others were feeling sleepy and could not see each other.

Bhishma (CE 92:77-79, GP 96:78-80)

तेषु श्रान्तेषु भग्नेषु मृदितेषु च भारत |

रात्रिः समभवद्घोरा नापश्याम ततो रणम् ||७७||

ततोऽवहारं सैन्यानां प्रचक्रुः कुरुपाण्डवाः |
घोरे निशामुखे रौद्रे वर्तमाने सुदारुणे ||७८||

अवहारं ततः कृत्वा सहिताः कुरुपाण्डवाः |
न्यविशन्त यथाकालं गत्वा स्वशिबिरं तदा ||७९||

One must wait until the eighth day of the war to read descriptions of the moon - the war scenes and their comparison with the moon. Duryodhana who was surrounded by his servants with oil lamps in their hands, on his way to meet Bhishma, is compared with the moon surrounded by planets.

Bhishma (CE 93:30-31, GP 97:31-32)

प्रदीपैः काञ्चनैस्तत्र गन्धतैलावसेचनैः |
परिवव्रुर्महात्मानं प्रज्वलद्भिः समन्ततः ||३०||

स तैः परिवृतो राजा प्रदीपैः काञ्चनैः शुभैः |
शुशुभे चन्द्रमा युक्तो दीप्तैरिव महाग्रहैः ||३१||

4.2.1.9 9th Day of the War

The fierce fighting began when the sun was ready to set on the western horizon, on the ninth day of the war.

Bhishma (CE 101:33, GP 105:35)

ततो युद्धं महाघोरं प्रावर्तत सुदारुणम् |
अपरां दिशमास्थाय द्योतमाने दिवाकरे ||३३||

The sun set while Bhishma was fiercely killing the Pandava army, and the entire army, utterly exhausted, was hoping for the fight to cease.

Bhishma (CE 102:78, GP 106:85)

विमृद्नतस्तस्य तु पाण्डुसेना; मस्तं जगामाथ सहस्ररश्मिः |
ततो बलानां श्रमकर्शितानां; मनोऽवहारं प्रति सम्बभूव ||७८||

It is not clear when exactly the fighting stopped, for all Sanjaya tells Dhritarashtra is that he did not <u>observe</u> the fighting after this time.

Bhishma (CE 103:1, GP 107:1)

युध्यतामेव तेषां तु भास्करेऽस्तमुपागते |
सन्ध्या समभवद्घोरा नापश्याम ततो रणम् ||१||

However, it appears that fighting stopped soon after.

Bhishma (CE 103:2-6, GP 107:2-6)

ततो युधिष्ठिरो राजा सन्ध्यां संदृश्य भारत |
वध्यमानं बलं चापि भीष्मेणामित्रघातिना ||२||

मुक्तशस्त्रं परावृत्तं पलायनपरायणम् |

भीष्मं च युधि संरब्धमनुयान्तं महारथान् ||३||

सोमकांश्च जितान्दृष्ट्वा निरुत्साहान्महारथान् |
चिन्तयित्वा चिरं ध्यात्वा अवहारमरोचयत् ||४||

ततोऽवहारं सैन्यानां चक्रे राजा युधिष्ठिरः |
तथैव तव सैन्यानामवहारो ह्यभूत्तदा ||५||

ततोऽवहारं सैन्यानां कृत्वा तत्र महारथाः |
न्यविशन्त कुरुश्रेष्ठ सङ्ग्रामे क्षतविक्षताः ||६||

4.2.1.10 10th Day of the War

On this day, Arjuna troubling Dusshasan, during the fight, is compared with angry *Rahu* troubling the Moon.

Bhishma (CE 106:35, GP 110:37)

दुःशासनं ततः क्रुद्धः पीडयामास पाण्डवः |
पर्वणीव सुसंक्रुद्धो राहु रुग्रो निशाकरम् ||३५||

दुःशासनं ततः क्रुद्धः पीडयामास पाण्डवः |
पर्वणीव सुसंक्रुद्धो राहुः पूर्ण निशाकरम् ||३७||

The Moon was described as rising with its pointed ends directed downwards, on the 10th day of the war.

84

ASTRONOMY EVIDENCE

Bhishma (CE 108:12, GP 112:12)

अपसव्यं ग्रहाश्चक्रुरलक्ष्माणं निशाकरम् |
अवाक्षिराश्च भगवानुदतिष्ठत चन्द्रमाः ||१२||

The rising of the Moon with its pointed (non-smooth) ends downward corroborates well with the rising (or visible) moon during 'Shukla paksha' of any month, i.e., bright half of the lunar month.

While Bhishma killed many warriors on the battlefield, his entire body was filled with arrows. The sun was ready to set on the western horizon and Bhishma fell on the ground. However, since his body was covered with arrows, it did not touch the ground. Bhishma noticed that the sun was still in "Dakshinayan," and when he heard the voice wondering how come Bhishma decided to die during "Dakshinayan," he murmured that he was still alive.

Bhishma (CE 114:80-89, GP 119:86-97)

अभिहत्य शरौघैस्तं शतशोऽथ सहस्रशः |
न तस्यासीदनिर्भिन्नं गात्रेष्वङ्गुलमात्रकम् ||८०||

एवं विभो तव पिता शरैर्विशकलीकृतः |
शिताग्रैः फल्गुनेनाजौ प्राक्षिराः प्रापतद्रथात् ||८१||
किञ्चिच्छेषे दिनकरे पुत्राणां तव पश्यताम् ||८१||

हा हेति दिवि देवानां पार्थिवानां च सर्वशः |
पतमाने रथाद्भीष्मे बभूव सुमहान्स्वनः ||८२||

तं पतन्तमभिप्रेक्ष्य महात्मानं पितामहम् |
सह भीष्मेण सर्वेषां प्रापतन्हृदयानि नः ||८३||

85

स पपात महाबाहुर्वसुधामनुनादयन्।
इन्द्रध्वज इवोत्सृष्टः केतुः सर्वधनुष्मताम् ||८४||
धरणीं नास्पृशच्चापि शरसङ्घैः समाचितः ||८४||

शरतल्पे महेष्वासं शयानं पुरुषर्षभम् ।
रथात्प्रपतितं चैनं दिव्यो भावः समाविशत् ||८५||

अभ्यवर्षत पर्जन्यः प्राकम्पत च मेदिनी ।
पतन्स दद्दशे चापि खर्वितं च दिवाकरम् ||८६||

सञ्ज्ञां चैवालभद्वीरः कालं सञ्चिन्त्य भारत ।
अन्तरिक्षे च शुश्राव दिव्यां वाचं समन्ततः ||८७||

कथं महात्मा गाङ्गेयः सर्वशस्त्रभृतां वरः ।
कालं कर्ता नरव्याघ्रः सम्प्राप्ते दक्षिणायने ||८८||

स्थितोऽस्मीति च गाङ्गेयस्तच्छ्रुत्वा वाक्यमब्रवीत् ।
धारयामास च प्राणान्पतितोऽपि हि भूतले ||८९||
उत्तरायणमन्विच्छन्भीष्मः कुरुपितामहः ||८९||

Bhishma was determined to stay alive, with the help of a boon at his disposal, by stating that he will remain alive until the sun turned northward, i.e., until the day of the winter solstice.

Bhishma (CE 114:96-100, GP 119:103-109)

तानब्रवीच्छान्तनवो नाहं गन्ता कथञ्चन ।
दक्षिणावृत आदित्ये एतन्मे मनसि स्थितम् ||९६||

गमिष्यामि स्वकं स्थानमासीद्यन्मे पुरातनम् |
उदगावृत्त आदित्ये हंसाः सत्यं ब्रवीमि वः ||९७||

धारयिष्याम्यहं प्राणानुत्तरायणकाङ्क्षया |
ऐश्वर्यभूतः प्राणानामुत्सर्गे नियतो ह्यहम् ||९८||
तस्मात्प्राणान्धारयिष्ये मुमूर्षुरुदगायने ||९८|

यश्च दत्तो वरो मह्यं पित्रा तेन महात्मना |
छन्दतो मृत्युरित्येवं तस्य चास्तु वरस्तथा ||९९||

धारयिष्ये ततः प्राणानुत्सर्गे नियते सति |
इत्युक्त्वा तांस्तदा हंसानशेत शरतल्पगः ||१००||

When Bhishma was surrounded by Arjuna and others, Bhishma stated that staying on this bed of arrows was appropriate for a kshatriya and re-iterated his decision to stay in that condition until the sun turned northward (i.e., until the day of the winter solstice). He asked the assembled kings to create a protective moat around him while he waited for the day of the winter solstice.

Bhishma (CE 115:46-50, GP 120:49—54)

एवमेतन्महाबाहो धर्मेषु परिनिष्ठितम् |
स्वप्तव्यं क्षत्रियेणाजौ शरतल्पगतेन वै ||४६||

एवमुक्त्वा तु बीभत्सुं सर्वास्तानब्रवीद्वचः |
राज्ञश्च राजपुत्रांश्च पाण्डवेनाभि संस्थितान् ||४७||

शयेयमस्यां शय्यायां यावदावर्तनं रवेः |

ये तदा पारयिष्यन्ति ते मां द्रक्ष्यन्ति वै नृपाः ||४८||

दिशं वैश्रवणाक्रान्तां यदा गन्ता दिवाकरः |
अर्चिष्मान्प्रतपँल्लोकान्नथेनोत्तमतेजसा ||४९||
विमोक्ष्येऽहं तदा प्राणान्सुहृदः सुप्रियानपि ||४९||
परिखा खन्यतामत्र ममावसदने नृपाः |
उपासिष्ये विवस्वन्तमेवं शरशताचितः ||५०||
उपारमध्वं सङ्ग्रामाद्वैराण्युत्सृज्य पार्थिवाः ||५०||

4.2.1.11 11th Day of the War

Drona became the head of Duryodhana's army. The day's battle ended when the sun set, and darkness set in.

Drona (CE 15:48-51, GP 16:49-53)

सूर्ये चास्तमनुप्राप्ते रजसा चाभिसंवृते |
नाज्ञायत तदा शत्रुर्न सुहृन्न च किञ्चन ||४८||

ततोऽवहारं चक्रुस्ते द्रोणदुर्योधनादयः |
तान्विदित्वा भृशं त्रस्तानयुद्धमनसः परान् ||४९||

स्वान्यनीकानि बीभत्सुः शनकैरवहारयत् |
ततोऽभितुष्टुवुः पार्थं प्रहृष्टाः पाण्डुसृञ्जयाः ||५०||
पाञ्चालाश्च मनोज्ञाभिर्वाग्भिः सूर्यमिवर्षयः ||५०||

एवं स्वशिबिरं प्रायाज्जित्वा शत्रून्धनञ्जयः |
पृष्ठतः सर्वसैन्यानां मुदितो वै सकेशवः ||७१||

Arjuna sitting in his chariot and surrounded by various jewels of his chariot on the 11th day of the war is compared with the moon surrounded by nakshatras.[49]

Drona (CE 15:52, GP 16:54)

मसारगल्वर्कसुवर्णरूप्यैः वैज्रप्रवालस्फटिकैश्च मुख्यैः |
चित्रे रथे पाण्डुसुतो बभासे; नक्षत्रचित्रे वियतीव चन्द्रः ||५२||

4.2.1.12 12th Day of the War

The descriptions of the war on the 12th day compare the white canopy on the chariot of the king Bhagadatta with the "full moon near nakshatra Krittika."

Drona (CE 19:18, GP 20:17)

माल्यदामवता राजा श्वेतच्छत्रेण धार्यता |
कृत्तिकायोगयुक्तेन पौर्णमास्यामिवेन्दुना ||१८||

Ashwatthama killed King Neel on this day and the face of King Neel looked like the "full moon."

Drona (CE 30:26, GP 31:26)

सम्पूर्णचन्द्राभमुखः पद्मपत्रनिभेक्षणः |
प्रांशुरुत्पलगर्भाभो निहतो न्यपतत्क्षितौ ||२६||

Warriors on the both sides were utterly exhausted, and the fighting stopped with the sunset.

Drona (CE 31:77, GP 32:80)

ततो बले भृशलुलिते परस्परं; निरीक्षमाणे रुधिरौघसम्प्लुते |
दिवाकरेऽस्तङ्गिरिमास्थिते शनै; रुभे प्रयाते शिबिराय भारत ||७७||

4.2.1.13 13th Day of the War

Sindhu-naresh Jayadratha's chariot looked like "the moon in the sky" as he attacked Abhimanyu.

Drona (CE 42:4, GP 43:4)

श्वेतच्छत्रपताकाभिश्चामरव्यजनेन च |
स बभौ राजलिङ्गैस्तैस्तारापतिरिवाम्बरे ||४||

Abhimanyu fought bravely and killed many key warriors of the Kauravas. In the end, many warriors simultaneously attacked him and the son of Dushshasana hit Abhimanyu with a club. Abhimanyu fell to the ground.

Abhimanyu on the ground looked like the sun, set on the western horizon, and like <u>the eclipsed moon</u> or like the dried ocean. Abhimanyu's face looked like <u>the full moon</u>.

Drona (CE 48:16-17, GP 49:17-18)

विमृद्य तरुशृङ्गाणि संनिवृत्तमिवानिलम् |
अस्तं गतमिवादित्यं तप्त्वा भारतवाहिनीम् ||१६||

उपप्लुतं यथा सोमं संशुष्कमिव सागरम् |
पूर्णचन्द्राभवदनं काकपक्षवृताक्षकम् ||१७||

Many warriors expressed their displeasure at the way Abhimanyu was killed as he looked like a fallen moon from the sky. The battlefield looked like the sky with the <u>full moon</u> surrounded by stars.

Drona (CE 48:20, 22, GP 49:21, 23)

अभिक्रोशन्ति भूतानि अन्तरिक्षे विशां पते |
दृष्ट्वा निपतितं वीरं च्युतं चन्द्रमिवाम्बरात् ||२०||

तस्मिंस्तु निहते वीरे बह्वशोभत मेदिनी |
द्यौर्यथा पूर्णचन्द्रेण नक्षत्रगणमालिनी ||२२||

Kaurva army, tired and exhausted, retreated to their camps while the Pandava warriors stood in sadness as the sun set on the western horizon.

Drona (CE 48:39-42, GP 50:1-4)

वयं तु प्रवरं हत्वा तेषां तैः शरपीडिताः |

निवेशायाभ्युपायाम सायाह्ने रुधिरोक्षिताः ||३९||

निरीक्षमाणास्तु वयं परे चायोधनं शनैः |
अपयाता महाराज ग्लानिं प्राप्ता विचेतसः ||४०||

ततो निशाया दिवसस्य चाशिवः; शिवारूतः सन्धिरवर्तताद्भुतः |
कुशेशयापीडनिभे दिवाकरे; विलम्बमानेऽस्तमुपेत्य पर्वतम् ||४१||

वरासिशक्त्यृष्टिवरूथचर्मणां; विभूषणानां च समाक्षिपन्प्रभाम् |
दिवं च भूमिं च समानयन्निव; प्रियां तनुं भानुरुपैति पावकम् ||४२||

4.2.1.14 14th Day of the War

Arjuna fought bravely and killed Jayadratha by the end of the day. Seven Kaurava brothers attacked Bhima and the scene looked like seven planets attacking the moon.

Drona (CE 112.22, GP 137:22)

तेऽपीडयन्भीमसेनं क्रुद्धाः सप्त महारथाः |
प्रजासंहरणे राजन्सोमं सप्त ग्रहा इव ||२२||

The fighting continued throughout the night with a short break in between and then continued until the sunrise.

4.2.1.15 15th Day of the War

Dhrishtadyumna killed Drona and angry Ashwatthama defeated the Pandava army. The fighting continued throughout the day.

4.2.1.16 16th Day of the War

Karna headed Duryodhana's army. The fierce fighting resumed, and both parties killed warriors of the opposing side. The faces of these dead warriors looked like the <u>full moon</u>.

Karna (CE 8:3, GP 12:3)

पूर्णचन्द्रार्कपद्मानां कान्तित्विड्गन्धतः समैः ।
उत्तमाङ्गैर्नृसिंहानां नृसिंहास्तस्तरुर्महीम् ॥३॥

Arjuna killed many "samshaptak" warriors and generated a pile of their bodies. These faces appeared like <u>the full moon</u>.

Karna (CE 12:4, GP 16:5)

शिरांस्युन्मथ्य वीराणां शितैर्भल्लैर्धनञ्जयः ।
पूर्णचन्द्राभवक्त्राणि स्वक्षिभ्रूदशनानि च ॥४॥
सन्तस्तार क्षितिं क्षिप्रं विनालैर्नलिनैरिव ॥४॥

93

ASTRONOMY EVIDENCE

The battlefield was soon covered with the <u>full-moon</u>-like faces of warriors. These scenes looked like a spread of lotuses and other flowers and like the starry sky of the sharad season.

Karna (CE 14:50, GP 19:49-50)

चन्द्रनक्षत्रभासैश्च वदनैश्चारुकुण्डलैः |
कॢप्तश्मश्रुभिरत्यर्थं वीराणां समलङ्कृतैः ||५०||
वदनैः पश्य सञ्छन्नां महीं शोणितकर्दमाम् ||५०||

चन्द्रनक्षत्रभासैश्च वदनैश्चारुकुण्डलैः ||४९||
कॢप्तश्मश्रुभिराकीर्णी पूर्णचन्द्रनिभैर्महीम् |

Karna (GP 19:50-51)

कुमुदोत्पलपद्मानां खण्डैः फुल्लं यथा सरः ||५०||

तथा महीभृतां वक्त्रैः कुमुदोत्पलसंनिभैः |
तारागणविचित्रस्य निर्मलेन्दुद्युतित्विषः ||५१||

पश्येमां नभसस्तुल्यां शरन्नक्षत्रमालिनीम् |

Ashwatthama killed the king of Pandya and the face of the king looked like the moon between two "Vishakha" nakshatra.

Karna (CE 15:42, GP 20:48)

शिरश्च तत्पूर्णशशिप्रभाननं; सरोषताम्रायतनेत्रमुन्नसम् |
क्षितौ विबभ्राज पतत्सकुण्डलं; विशाखयोर्मध्यगतः शशी यथा ||४२||

The fallen faces on the battlefield appeared like the <u>full moon</u>. They also appeared like the stars in the sky.

Karna (CE 19:28, GP 27:34)

सकुण्डलानि स्वक्षीणि पूर्णचन्द्रनिभानि च |
शिरांस्युर्व्यामदृश्यन्त तारागण इवाम्बरे ||२८||

The dust and the setting of the sun created darkness. Warriors were terrified of fighting during the night, so they returned to their camps.

Karna (CE 21:35-41, GP 30:37-43)

एवं तेषां तदा युद्धे संसक्तानां जयैषिणाम् |
गिरिमस्तं समासाद्य प्रत्यपद्यत भानुमान् ||३५||
तमसा च महाराज रजसा च विशेषतः |
न किञ्चित्प्रत्यपश्याम शुभं वा यदि वाशुभम् ||३६||

ते त्रसन्तो महेष्वासा रात्रियुद्धस्य भारत |
अपयानं ततश्चक्रुः सहिताः सर्ववाजिभिः ||३७||
कौरवेषु च यातेषु तदा राजन्दिनक्षये |
जयं सुमनसः प्राप्य पार्थाः स्वशिबिरं ययुः ||३८||

वादित्रशब्दैर्विविधैः सिंहनादैश्च नर्तितैः |
परानवहसन्तश्च स्तुवन्तश्चाच्युतार्जुनौ ||३९||

कृतेऽवहारे तैर्वीरैः सैनिकाः सर्व एव ते |
आशिषः पाण्डवेयेषु प्रायुज्यन्त नरेश्वराः ||४०||

ततः कृतेऽवहारे च प्रहृष्टाः कुरुपाण्डवाः |
निशायां शिबिरं गत्वा न्यविशन्त नरेश्वराः ||४१||

4.2.1.17 17th Day of the War

The fighting resumed with the sunrise and Arjuna went on defeating various kings, and the battlefield filled with the faces of fallen kings looked like the <u>full moon.</u>

Karna (GP 46:62)

विशालायतताम्राक्षैः पूर्णचन्द्रनिभाननैः |
एषा भूः कीर्यते राज्ञां शिरोभिरपलायिनाम् ||६२||

Dhrishtadyumna was protected by the five sons of Draupadi, and the scene looked like the moon protected by five bright stars.

Karna (CE 32:6, GP 47:6)

पार्षतं त्वभि सन्तस्थुर्द्रौपदेया युयुत्सवः |
सानुगा भीमवपुषश्चन्द्रं तारागणा इव ||६||

पार्षतं जुगुपुः सर्वे द्रौपदेया युयुत्सवः|
दिव्यवर्मायुधधराः शार्दूलमसविक्रमाः ||६||
सानुगा दीप्तवपुषश्चन्द्रं तारागणा इव |

Yudhishthira's chariot was protected by two Panchal warriors, and the scene looked like the moon protected by two Punarvasus.

Karna (CE 33:15-16, GP 49:27-28)

ततः क्षुराभ्यां पाञ्चाल्यौ चक्ररक्षौ महात्मनः |
जघान समरे शूरः शरैः संनतपर्वभिः ||१५||
तावुभौ धर्मराजस्य प्रवीरौ परिपार्श्वतः |
रथाभ्याशे चकाशेते चन्द्रस्येव पुनर्वसू ||१६||

ततः क्षुराभ्यां पाञ्चाल्यौ चक्ररक्षौ महात्मनः |
जघान चन्द्रदेवं च दण्डधारं च संयुगे ||२७||

तावुभौ धर्मराजस्य प्रवीरौ परिपार्श्वतः |
रथाभ्याशे चकाशेते चन्द्रस्येव पुनर्वसू ||२८||

Bhima killed Vivitsu and the face of fallen Vivitsu looked like the _full moon_.

Karna (CE 35:11, GP 51:12)

विवित्सोस्तु ततः क्रुद्धो भल्लेनापाहरच्छिरः |
सकुण्डलशिरस्त्राणं पूर्णचन्द्रोपमं तदा ||११||

भीमेन च महाराज स पपात हतो भुवि ||११||

Arjuna killed the younger brother of King Sudakshina, king of Kambhoja, and the face of this fallen warrior looked like the _full moon._

Karna (CE 40:104, GP 56:111)

अस्यास्यतोऽर्धचन्द्राभ्यां स बाहू परिघोपमौ |
पूर्णचन्द्राभवक्त्रं च क्षुरेणाभ्यहनच्छिरः ||१०४||

Karna looked like the moon on the eastern horizon and the canopy of Karna's chariot looked like the <u>full moon</u>.

Karna (CE 43:38-39, GP 60:40-41)

पश्य कर्णं रणे पार्थं श्वेतच्छविविराजितम् |
उदयं पर्वतं यद्वच्छोभयन्वै दिवाकरः ||३८||
पूर्णचन्द्रनिकाशेन मूर्ध्नि छत्रेण भारत |
ध्रियमाणेन समरे तथा शतशलाकिना ||३९||

पश्य कर्णं रणे पार्थं श्वेतच्छत्रविराजितम् |
उदयं पर्वतं यद्वच्छशाङ्केनाभिशोभितम् |
पूर्णचन्द्रनिकाशेन मूर्ध्निच्छत्रेण भारत |
ध्रियमाणेन समरे श्रीमच्छतशलाकिना ||४१||

Bhima looked like the <u>full moon</u>, surrounded by Kaurava warriors.

Karna (CE 55:33-34, GP 77:33-35)

स तैः परिवृतः शूरैः शूरो राजन्समन्ततः |
शुशुभे भरतश्रेष्ठ नक्षत्रैरिव चन्द्रमाः ||३३||
स रराज तथा सङ्ख्ये दर्शनीयो नरोत्तमः |
निर्विशेषं महाराज यथा हि विजयस्तथा ||३४||

स तैः परिवृतः शूरैः शूरो राजन् समन्ततः ||३३||
शुशुभे भरतश्रेष्ठो नक्षत्रैरिव चन्द्रमाः |
परिवेषी यथा सोमः परिपूर्णो विराजते ||३४||
स रराज तथा संख्ये दर्शनीयो नरोत्तमः |
निर्विशेषो महाराज यथा हि विजयस्तथा ||३५||

The Pandava army felt happy to see Yudhishthira return to the battlefield, not unlike the joy people feel when they see the moon coming out of the eclipse.

Karna (GP 89:71)

तथोपयातं युधि धर्मराजं; दृष्ट्वा मुदा सर्वभूतान्यनन्दन् ||७१||
राहोर्विमुक्तं विमलं समग्रं; चन्द्रं यथैवाभ्युदितं तथैव |

Arjuna killed Karna towards the end of the day and Karna's face, fallen on the ground, looked like the mid-day sun of sharad season.

Karna (CE 67:24, GP 91:52)

तदुद्यतादित्यसमानवर्चसं; शरन्नभोमध्यगभास्करोपमम् |
वराङ्गमुर्व्यामपतच्चमूपते; दिवाकरोऽस्तादिव रक्तमण्डलः ||२४||

Karna's face, fallen on the ground, looked like the <u>full moon</u>.

Karna (GP 94:37)

चारुवेषधरं वीरं चारुमौलिशिरोधरम् |
तन्मुखं सूतपुत्रस्य पूर्णचन्द्रसमद्युति ||३७||

ASTRONOMY EVIDENCE

The sun set after the death of Karna.

Karna (CE 68:47, GP 94:49)

हते स्म कर्णे सरितो न स्रवन्ति; जगाम चास्तं कलुषो दिवाकरः |
ग्रहश्च तिर्यग्ज्वलितार्कवर्णो; यमस्य पुत्रोऽभ्युदियाय राजन् ||४७||

Krishna and Arjuna returned to their camp. Kaurava warriors
ran away from the battlefield, terrified and exhausted. Bhima and
other warriors chased them and fighting continued. Kripacharya
persuaded Duryodhana to stop the fight and ask forgiveness from
Yudhishthira. Duryodhana decided to continue the fight, and all
Kaurava warriors returned to the battlefield and spent the night on
the battlefield.

Shalya (CE 5:1-3, GP 6:1-3)

अथ हैमवते प्रस्थे स्थित्वा युद्धाभिनन्दिनः |
सर्व एव महाराज योधास्तत्र समागताः ||१||

शल्यश्च चित्रसेनश्च शकुनिश्च महारथः |
अश्वत्थामा कृपश्चैव कृतवर्मा च सात्वतः ||२||

सुषेणोऽरिष्टसेनश्च धृतसेनश्च वीर्यवान् |
जयत्सेनश्च राजानस्ते रात्रिमुषितास्ततः ||३||

Duryodhana made Shalya the leader of his army. They did not
return to their camps, and instead slept on the battlefield.

Shalya (CE 5:18-19, GP 6:19-20)

अयं कुलेन वीर्येण तेजसा यशसा श्रिया |
सर्वैर्गुणैः समुदितः शल्यो नोऽस्तु चमूपतिः ||१८||

भागिनेयान्निजांस्त्यक्त्वा कृतज्ञोऽस्मानुपागतः |
महासेनो महाबाहुर्महासेन इवापरः ||१९||

Shalya (CE 6:20, GP 7:23)

प्रहर्षं प्राप्य सेना तु तावकी भरतर्षभ |
तां रात्रिं सुखिनी सुप्ता स्वस्थचित्तेव साभवत् ||२०||

4.2.1.18 18th Day of the War

When the night was over, Duryodhana asked his warriors to be ready.

Shalya (CE 7:1, GP 8:1)

व्यतीतायां रजन्यां तु राजा दुर्योधनस्तदा |
अब्रवीतावकान्सर्वान्संनह्यन्तां महारथाः ||१||

Duryodhana was standing in the middle of the battlefield surrounded by his bodyguards, and the canopy of his chariot looked like the full moon.

101

Shalya (CE 23:4, GP 24:4)

यत्रैतत्सुमहच्छत्रं पूर्णचन्द्रसमप्रभम् |
यत्रैते सतलत्राणा रथास्तिष्ठन्ति दंशिताः ||४||

Duryodhana, fallen in the battlefield and surrounded by dust, looked like the <u>full moon</u> surrounded by ring of darkness.

Shalya (CE 64:6, GP 65:6-7)

महावातसमुत्थेन संशुष्कमिव सागरम् |
पूर्णचन्द्रमिव व्योम्नि तुषारावृतमण्डलम् ||६||

Duyrodhana sent the message and made Ashwatthama the leader of his side. While Ashwatthama left, along with Kripacharya and Kritavarma, Duryodhana stayed lying on the ground through the night.

Shalya (CE 64:40-43, GP 65:43-46)

राजस्तु वचनं श्रुत्वा कृपः शारद्वतस्ततः |
द्रौणिं राज्ञो नियोगेन सेनापत्येऽभ्यषेचयत् ||४०||

सोऽभिषिक्तो महाराज परिष्वज्य नृपोत्तमम् |
प्रययौ सिंहनादेन दिशः सर्वा विनादयन् ||४१||

दुर्योधनोऽपि राजेन्द्र शोणितौघपरिप्लुतः |
तां निशां प्रतिपेदेऽथ सर्वभूतभयावहाम् ||४२||
अपक्रम्य तु ते तूर्णं तस्मादायोधनान्नृप |
शोकसंविग्नमनसश्चिन्ताध्यानपराभवन् ||४३||

Ashwatthama along with Kripacharya and Kritavarma attacked the Pandava camp at night, killing Shikhandi, Drishtadyumna, the five sons of Draupadi, and other warriors.

4.2.1.19 1st Day <u>After</u> the War Was Over

Bhima and Arjuna humbled Ashwatthama, and the Kuru women came to the battlefield searching for the bodies of their loved ones.

Gandhari compared faces of the Balhik king and Madraraj Shalya with the <u>full moon</u>.

Stri (CE 22:6, GP 22:6)

अतीव मुखवर्णोऽस्य निहतस्यापि शोभते ।
सोमस्येवाभिपूर्णस्य पौर्णमास्यां समुद्यतः ॥६॥

Stri (CE 23:4, GP 23:4)

अहो धिक्पश्य शल्यस्य पूर्णचन्द्रसुदर्शनम् ।
मुखं पद्मपलाशाक्षं वडैरादष्टमव्रणम् ॥४॥

4.2.2 Positions and Phases of the Moon

Let's emphasize the evidence of the phases of the moon through 18 days of the war in the context of 4 specific positions of the moon.

The first position refers to the "full-moon-like" moon on the 12th day of war, near nakshatra Krittika.

Drona (CE 19:18, GP 20:17)

माल्यदामवता राजा श्वेतच्छत्रेण धार्यता |
कृत्तिकायोगयुक्तेन पौर्णमास्यामिवेन्दुना ||१८||

The second position (2 references) refers to the moon, on the 16th day of the war (1) between Vishakha and (2) surrounded by 5 bright stars. Both descriptions can be interpreted to be near the point of nakshatra Ardra/Punarvasu (especially in the year 5561 BCE).

Karna (CE 15:42, GP 20:48)

शिरश्च तत्पूर्णशशिप्रभाननं; सरोषताम्रायतनेत्रमुन्नसम् |
क्षितौ विबभ्राज पतत्सकुण्डलं; विशाखयोर्मध्यगतः शशी यथा ||४२||

Karna (CE 32:6, GP 47:6)

पार्षतं त्वभि सन्तस्थुर्द्रौपदेया युयुत्सवः |
सानुगा भीमवपुषश्चन्द्रं तारागणा इव ||६||

पार्षतं जुगुपुः सर्वे द्रौपदेया युयुत्सवः|
दिव्यवर्मायुधधराः शार्दूलमसविक्रमाः ||६||
सानुगा दीप्तवपुषश्चन्द्रं तारागणा इव |

This hunch is further confirmed when we have a crisp reference to "moon near Punarvasu" on the 17th day of the war.

Karna (CE 33:15-16, GP 49:27-28)

ततः क्षुराभ्यां पाञ्चाल्यौ चक्ररक्षौ महात्मनः |
जघान समरे शूरः शरैः संनतपर्वभिः ||१५||
तावुभौ धर्मराजस्य प्रवीरौ परिपार्श्वतः |
रथाभ्याशे चकाशेते चन्द्रस्येव पुनर्वसू ||१६||

ततः क्षुराभ्यां पाञ्चाल्यौ चक्ररक्षौ महात्मनः |
जघान चन्द्रदेवं च दण्डधारं च संयुगे ||२७||
तावुभौ धर्मराजस्य प्रवीरौ परिपार्श्वतः |
रथाभ्याशे चकाशेते चन्द्रस्येव पुनर्वसू ||२८||

These references of positions and phases of the moon from 12th through 17th day of the war allow us to assert this as the lunar month of Margashirsha, and specifically Shukla paksha of the lunar month of Margashirsha.

This identification of 'Margashirsha Shukla paksha' is due to (1) the descriptions of the phases of the moon, 1st through 18th day of the war were of waxing fortnight and, (2) the fact that the full moon descriptions occur during positions of the moon near nakshatra Krittika through Punarvasu with nakshatra Mrigashirsha as the central nakshatra.

4.3 Lunar Calendar Evidence

ASTRONOMY EVIDENCE

4.3.1 Lower Limit on the First Day of the War

The Mahabharata text refers to Kartika as the full moon occurring prior to the first day of the Mahabharata war.

Bhishma (CE 2:23, GP 2:23)

अलक्ष्यः प्रभया हीनः पौर्णमासीं च कार्तिकीम् |
चन्द्रोऽभूदग्निवर्णश्च समवर्णे नभस्तले ||२३||

The Mahabharata text also refers to "Chaturdashi" of Vadya paksha (waning fortnight) occurring prior to the first day of the Mahabharata war.

Bhishma (CE 3:31, GP 3:31)

मांसवर्षं पुनस्तीव्रमासीत्कृष्णचतुर्दशीम् |
अर्धरात्रे महाघोरमतृप्यंस्तत्र राक्षसाः ||३१||

These two astronomy observations allow us to set "Kartika Amavasya" as the lower limit on the tithi for the first day of the war.

4.3.2 Upper Limit on the Day of Bhishma-nirvana

The Mahabharata text contains two references that allow us to set the upper limit not only on the tithi of Bhishma-nirvana but also the tithi for the first day of the war. Both references occur in Ashwamedha parva where references are made to the future event of Chaitra full moon day. Vyasa tells Yudhishthira that the latter would be given "diksha" of Ashwamedha yajna on the "upcoming" Chaitra full moon day.

Ashwamedhika (CE 71:4, GP 72:4)

चैत्र्यां हि पौर्णमास्यां च तव दीक्षा भविष्यति |
सम्भाराः सम्भ्रियन्तां ते यज्ञार्थं पुरुषर्षभ ||४||

Arjuna asked King Vajradatta of Pragjyotisha to arrive in Hastinapura on the day of Chaitra full moon when Ashwamedha yajna was scheduled to take place.

Ashwamedhika (CE 75:25, GP 76:25)

आगच्छेथा महाराज परां चैत्रीमुपस्थिताम् |
तदाश्वमेधो भविता धर्मराजस्य धीमतः ||२५||

Summary

(1) Most of the 18 days of the Mahabharata war took place during the first part (first month) of the Sharad season.
(2) The Mahabharata war began around Amavasya (+/- one day) and ended three to four days after the full moon day, i.e., the war began and took place during the Shukla paksha (waxing phase) of the lunar month.
(3) The Mahabharata war indeed began with the day of Amavasya and took place during the lunar month of Margashirsha.
(4) The inference of war beginning with Amavasya, and thus taking place during the Shukla paksha of the lunar month of Margashirsha is further validated by references to the occurrence of Kartika Purnima and Kartika Krishna Chaturdashi prior to the first day of the Mahabharata war.
(5) The inference in (4) is further corroborated by occurrence of Chaitra Purnima, long after the day of Bhishma-nirvana.

5

Astronomy Agama

"Consequently, he who wishes to attain to human perfection, must therefore first study Logic, next the various branches of Mathematics in their proper order, then Physics, and lastly Metaphysics."
- Maimonides

We will cover a few astronomy concepts that are relevant for chronology and sensitivity (errors) calculations of Bhishma-nirvana.

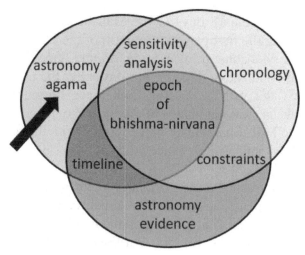

5.1 Celestial Time Clock

Let's begin with the analogy of "mechanical clock and its

mechanism" with that of the "celestial clock." Various celestial motions are like the motions of various gears of the wheel train of a mechanical clock.

Power   Wheel Train   Display

Escapement

While a power spring is the source of power that moves the wheel train in a mechanical clock, the gravitational forces and the interplay between them are responsible for motions of the moon around the earth, motions of the earth, and the precession of equinoxes.

We carefully control the settings of the wheel train and escapement mechanism in order to generate precise and accurate time on the display of a mechanical clock. In the case of "Archeo-astronomy," the task is to interpret "astronomy observations" in the context of the celestial clock in order to predict precise and accurate timing of either an ancient document containing those astronomy observations or ancient structure that was supposedly aligned according to astronomy coordinates of that time.

The celestial clock appears complex and it is, but so does a mechanical clock to a novice. On the other hand, a little patience and some willingness to comprehend the details is all that is required to understand both.

Let's understand this celestial clock. The sun and the path of the sun as it appears to go around the earth (ecliptic) is the reference point and the reference frame for our celestial clock. Thus, we will begin with the sun and the solar year.

5.1.1 Solar Year

The solar year is the time interval required for the earth to make one complete revolution around the sun, measured from one vernal equinox to the next. This time interval is equal to 365 days, 5 hours, 48 minutes, and 45.51 seconds. It is represented by a Gregorian calendar with 12 months and length of 365 days, unless it is a leap year when the length is 366 days. While the first day of the year in Gregorian calendar is arbitrary, in the sense that it does not coincide with any specific cardinal point, the Gregorian calendar has rules so that it closely approximates the solar year and will continue to do so for the next 8000 years without introducing much inaccuracy. The focus of this popular solar calendar (Gregorian) to align the four days of cardinal points and keep them fixed by making appropriate corrections (when required) with the dates determined (e.g., 21 June and 21 December, 23 March and 23 September).

Solar months are 12 in number in the Gregorian calendar system, and the length of each month is arbitrarily set so that all days of the year together add up to 365.

5.1.2 Solar Day

It is defined as "the length of time" that elapses for the sun to reach its highest point in the sky two consecutive times. This duration is approximately 24 hours. This is our most familiar "24-hour" day. Inventions of mechanical and now digital clocks allow us to measure it from any arbitrary reference point, such as midnight, as is done in our times.

5.1.3 Solar Month

True solar month would/should refer to the time interval when the sun stays in the region of a specific zodiac. However, this method is not followed by any existing solar calendars. In that sense, duration and names of solar months (January through December) of Gregorian calendar are arbitrary.

5.2 Lunar Cycles

5.2.1 Lunar Year

The moon takes 27.3 days to make a complete round trip around the earth. However, the earth itself moves by a significant distance during this time, and thus it takes the moon around 29.5 days to reach the same phase with respect to the earth. This is the lunar month.

The length of time for the moon to make one revolution in its orbit is difficult to predict and varies from its average value. Because observations are subject to uncertainty and weather conditions, and astronomical methods are highly complex, there have been attempts to create fixed arithmetical rules. The average length of the synodic month is 29.530589 days.

The lunar year is made up of 12 such lunar months, and thus the length of the lunar year is equal to 354 (29.5 x 12 = 354) days.

The Islamic calendar follows the lunar year. Since the lunar year is shorter by 10-11 days from the solar year, Islamic holidays occur 10-11 days earlier each subsequent year. For example, the month of Ramadan occurs earlier by a month (with respect to the solar calendar) every three years. This also means if the month of Ramadan occurs during the peak of winter in any given year (Gregorian calendar), it will occur at the peak of summer 18 years in the future.

5.2.2 Tithi (Lunar Day)

In the Indian calendar system (luni-solar year) a tithi is a lunar

111

day or the time it takes for the longitudinal angle between the moon and the sun to increase by 12^0. Tithi begins at varying times of the day and vary in duration from 19 to 26 hours.

There are 30 tithis in each lunar month. Amavasya is new moon (no moon) day. It is followed by Pratipada (1), Dwitiya (2), Tritiya (3), Chaturthi (4), Panchami (5), Shashthi (6), Saptami (7), Ashtami (8), Navami (9), Dashami (10), Ekadashi (11), Dwadashi (12), Trayodashi (13), Chaturdashi (14) and Purnima (Full moon day). These tithis are repeated for the second half of the lunar month, beginning with Pratipada, Dwitiya, etc. and end with Amavasya when a new lunar month begins.

The Mahabharata method of referring to the day is by referring to the nakshatra closest to the moon. One can determine the lunar month with reasonable accuracy by knowing the nakshatra of the day along with the paksha and the phase of the moon.

The lunar day (tithi) and the nakshatra of the day is not the same as the day defined by the rising and setting of the sun. The lunar day (tithi) and/or nakshatra of the day could be determined by simply noting down the phase of the moon and/or nakshatra close to the position of the moon. The lunar day (tithi) can also be calculated mathematically. The timing of an observation and an error on the part of an observer may lead to an error of +/- one day (i.e., lunar day or nakshatra) in noting down the phase or position of the moon.

In the Indian calendar system, "Aha" may refer to a time interval when the sun is above the horizon, "Ratra" may refer to the time interval when the sun is below the horizon and "AhoRatra" as referring to the modern "24-hour" day. It is important to note that the words "aham" or "ratra" were also used to designate a "24-hour day" in Mahabharata times. A day was further divided into Muhurtas (30 Muhurta = 1 day = 24 hours), which were in turn further divided into smaller units.

5.2.3 Nakshatra (Wives of the Moon)

The predictable rising of the sun provided the ancients a unit of time. However, to track the progress of time, one aspires to monitor the motion of a moving object with respect to non-moving objects (non-moving only in a relative sense since all astral bodies are in motion). Observations of the moon's position (moving) with respect to those of nakshatras (not moving) at night provided such an opportunity. Astronomers of the Mahabharata era used the system of "Nakshatra-Ganana," developed by their predecessors to keep track of time.

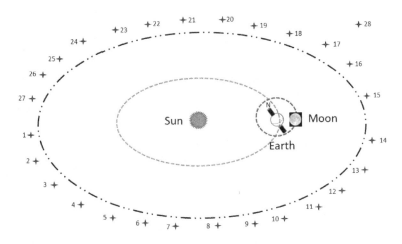

A nakshatra, which is loosely translated as "asterism," could be either a specific star (e.g., Chitra) or a group of stars (e.g., Krittika) along the ecliptic and is employed as a reference in noting down the positions of astral bodies (sun, moon, planets, comets, etc.).

Additional evidence is emerging from the pages of ancient Indian narratives that allude to varying number of nakshtras, employed by ancient Indian astronomers. However, the logic and rationale behind such varied systems is not clear at this time. What is clear is that the epics have made used of the nakshatra system with 27 (or 28) nakshatras. The average angular space for nakshatra was mathematically defined based on the 360 degrees divided by the number of nakshttras assumed in the system.

Table 1 Nakshatra, Nakshatra Devata, Modern star, RA, and Dec (5561 BCE)

Nakshatra	Yoga Tara	Nakshatra Devata	RA	DEC	Nirayan	Sayan
			arc-sec	arc-sec	(Vartak)	(Vartak)
Punarvasu	Pollux	Aditi	25,200	35,040	28	7
Pushya	Altarf	Brihaspati	81,900	(7,440)	1	8
Ashlesha	zeta Hydrae	Nagas/Sarpah	117,900	3,900	2	9
Magha	Regulus	Pitarah	156,600	61,800	3	10
Purva-Phalguni	Zosma	Aryaman (Bhaga)	180,000	120,480	4	11
Uttara Phalguni	Denebola	Bhaga (Aryaman)	229,500	124,980	5	12
Hasta	Algorab	Savitar (Sun?)	323,100	44,820	6	13
Chitra	Spica	Twastra (Indra)	361,800	79,380	7	14
Swati	Zeta Bootis	Vayu	381,600	213,360	8	15
Vishakha	Zubeneschamali	Indragni	469,800	102,180	9	16
Anuradha	Dschubba	Mitra	506,700	52,800	10	17
Jyeshtha	Antares	Indra (Varuna)	528,300	35,580	11	18
Moola	Shaula	Pitarah (Nirriti)	566,100	(14,160)	12	19
Purva-Ashadha	Kaus Australis	Apah	603,900	(19,140)	13	20
Uttara-Ashadha	Nunki	Visve Devah	639,000	(5,100)	14	21
Shravana	Altair	Vishnu	745,200	74,040	15	22
(Abhijit)	Vega	Brahma	784,800	193,320	16	23
Dhanishtha	Sualocin	Vasavah	802,800	67,260	17	24
Shatabhisaj (Shatataraka?)	Sadalmelik	Indra (Varuna)	828,000	(25,980)	18	25
Purva-Bhadrapada	Markab	Aja Ekapad	902,700	(10,500)	19	26
Uttara-Bhadrapada	Algenib	Ahir-Budhnya	954,900	(41,100)	20	27
Revati	Kullat Nunu	Pusan	1,019,700	(66,240)	21	28
Ashwini	Hamal	Asvinau	1,056,600	(44,040)	22	1
Bharani	41 Arietis	Yama	1,094,400	(35,820)	23	2
Krittika	Pleiades	Agni	1,143,000	(47,880)	24	3
Rohini	Aldebaran	Prajapati	1,188,000	(68,040)	25	4
Mriga- shirshya	Bellatrix	Soma	1,245,600	(92,040)	26	5
Ardra	Betelgeuse	Rudra	1,270,800	(78,480)	27	6

It appears that the desired number of nakshatras were determined based on how long it took the moon to complete one orbital cycle. Since the moon completes one cycle through its orbit in 27.3 days, 27 nakshatras were selected. This nakshatra system was also used to track positions of other astral bodies. Since the moon visited each nakshatra once every month, poetically, it was perceived as moon visiting each of his 27 wives each day of the month, until the moon visited all of them, only to repeat the cycle during the next month. These wives of the moon were given specific names, were assigned a devata (deity), and are frequently referred to by the name of their assigned deity. The nakshatras, along with their yoga tara and nakshatra deity, are listed in Table 1.

Some nakshatras have synonyms and were recognized by those synonyms, in addition to being referred to by their presiding deity.

For example, "Bhadrapada" is also called "Proshtha-pada," "Dhanishtha" is also called "Shravishtha" and "Shatabhisaj" is called "Shata-taraka." Some variations can also be seen while assigning a presiding deity to a given nakshatra. These variations, fortunately, do not lead to any confusion. Existence of other evidence and cross-references within Indian literature are sufficient to understand the nakshatra being referred to. The nakshatra closest to the moon on a given day is the "nakshatra of the day" in the Indian calendar system. Determination of the nakshatra of any given day based on visual observations can lead to an error of +/- one day.

5.2.4 Lunar Month

There are two definitions of lunar months - Purnamanta and Amanta. A lunar month that begins with the full moon day and ends on the next full moon day is called Purnamanta. A lunar month that begins on Amavasya (new moon day) and ends on the next Amavasya is called Amanta.

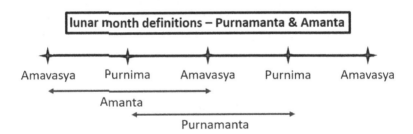

We will follow the definition of Amanta lunar month throughout the book. In the Amanta system, lunar months are named after the nakshatra near full moon during that month. Lunar months are named as Chaitra, Vaishakha, Jyeshtha, Ashadha, Shravana, Bhadrapada, Ashwin, Kartika, Margashirsha, Pausha, Magha, and Phalgun.

5.3 Luni-Solar Year

The Gregorian calendar and the Islamic calendar are examples of purely solar and purely lunar calendars, respectively. The Indian calendar is decidedly luni-solar from ancient times. The Indian Calendar does have regional variations; however, the core of it can be described without getting into regional nuances.

The basic unit of the Indian calendar is the lunar day (tithi). For the purposes of defining a year, the next unit of the Indian luni-solar calendar is the lunar month. The lunar month is the time interval either from one new moon to the next, or from one full moon to the next.

The Indian luni-solar calendar is "Nirayana" in nature. The Nirayana year is the time taken for the sun to return to the same fixed point on the ecliptic. The Nirayana year comprises 12 solar months. The lunar year consisting of 12 lunar months is shorter than the solar Nirayana year and hence Adhika masa (leap months) must be added periodically so that the calendar approximates the Nirayana solar year. The occurrence of Adhika masa is not (cannot be) determined by arithmetical rules of the Gregorian calendar. Additionally, some lunar months in the "Amanta" luni-solar calendar can have skipped days (tithi) or repeated days (tithi) which makes the numbering of days in the month slightly more complicated than usual.

Length of a lunar month = 29.5 days

Length of a lunar year = 12 x 29.5 = 354 days

Length of a solar year = 365.2422 ~ 365 days

Difference between solar and lunar year =
365-354 = 11 days.

5.3.1 Adhika Masa

Indian calendar makers came up with the ingenious idea of

"Adhika masa" (extra lunar month) to enable synchronization between the solar and the lunar year. While the method(s) to determine "Adhika masa" might have changed over the millenniums, the invention of "Adhika masa" is very old. Not only the Rig-Veda, but also the Mahabharata refers to "Adhika masa," and thus we have reason to believe in the existence of "Adhika masa" during Ramayana times, since the Ramayana is post Rig-Veda, but before the Mahabharata. I did not require the assumption of "Adhika masa" in my Ramayana research. Rather, the point I want to emphasize is that the existence of "Adhika masa" in calendar calculations during Ramayana times should not surprise us.

While references to "Adhika masa" exist in the Rig-Veda and the Mahabharata, no specific method to determine "Adhika masa" is mentioned. However, to clarify the concept of selection and naming of Adhika masa, I will illustrate the method employed in India in our times.

Recall that the lunar month begins with Amavasya (Amanta reckoning), and that the moon and the sun are together, as seen from the earth, on Amavasya day. The ecliptic path of the sun is divided into 12 zodiacs (27 nakshatras), and thus each zodiac is approximately 30^0 ($30^0/360^0$ or 1/12) of the ecliptic. This also means that on an average, the sun will travel through the area of each zodiac in approximately 30 days. The sun transiting from one zodiac into the next is called "Sankrantee" (San–Krantee: meaningful movement/transition).

Typically, Amavasya (new moon day) falls only once between two Sankrantees. However, occasionally, Amavasya may fall twice while the sun is still transiting through the area of a single zodiac. The lunar month defined by this second Amawasya is termed as Adhika masa.

Let us analyze the basis of Adhika masa calculations. The earth is revolving around the sun. The earth completes one circle around the sun in 365.2564 days (365 days, 6 hours, 9 minutes, and 12.96 seconds) whereas the moon takes 29.5306 days (29 days, 12 hours, 44 minutes, and 3.84 seconds) from new moon (Amavasya) to the next new moon (next Amavasya). Therefore, the duration of the lunar month is 29.5306 days, and the number of days in 12 lunar months is 29.5306 x 12 = 354.3672 days. The difference between a solar year and a lunar year is 10.8992 days ~ 11 days.

Therefore, every year, lunar months (and thus tithis) occur 11 days earlier. In three years, this difference reaches up to 33 days, which is more than one month. This difference necessitates insertion of an Adhika masa every ~ three years.

The timing of Adhika masa varies. It may come after an interval of 2 years and 4 months, 2 years and 9 months, 2 years and 10 months, or 2 years and 11 months. On average, an Adhika masa comes in 2 years and 8.5 months. This value can be verified by dividing the duration of a lunar month, i.e., 29.5 days by 10.9. A lunar year is 10.9 days shorter than a solar year, therefore, after dividing 29.53/10.9 = 2 years and 8.5 months, there arises a difference of one month.

5.3.2 Kshaya Masa

Recall that usually, Amavasya (new moon) falls once between two sankrantees, sankrantee being the sun's transit into the area of the next zodiac. On a rare occasion, no Amavasya would occur between two sankrantees, and when that happens, the subsequent lunar month is considered as Kshaya (elapsed). Let's us understand why this may happen.

The minimum value between two sankrantees is 29 days, 10 hours, and 48 minutes, and the maximum value is 31 days, 10 hours, and 48 minutes, whereas the minimum value between two Amavasyas (new moons) is 29 days, 5 hours, 54 minutes, and 14 seconds, and the maximum value between two new moons is 29 days, 19 hours, 36 minutes, and 29 seconds. Therefore, it so happens, although rarely, that no Amavasya (new moon) falls between two sankrantees. This generally happens after 19 years, or after 141 years, and sometimes after 65, 76, or 122 years. This type of situation is termed as Kshaya masa. This is possible during the sun's transit through zodiacs with smaller areas such as Scorpio, Sagittarius, and Capricorn. This implies that Kshaya masa most likely happens during the lunar months of Margashirsha,

Pausha, or Magha.

5.3.3 Why Synchronize Lunar and Solar Calendars?

While the tithi (lunar day) is a unit for daily measurement of time, and the lunar month is a unit for monthly measure of time, it is the solar year that determines the seasons. In agrarian cultures, the importance of synchronizing lunar and solar years is obvious. This is also true for a culture that is deep in commerce and distant navigation. Synchronizing lunar days and months with the solar year is critical for planting and harvesting of crops and ensuring safe navigation. Celebration of festivals, initiation and completion of Yajnas, and strict adherence to rituals on specific days of the year were all meant to informally educate the society and to aid in maintenance of the calendar.

5.4 Seasons (Ritu)

Six seasons were recognized with each season made up of approximately two lunar months. The seasons (Ritu) were designated as Vasanta (spring), Grishma (summer), Varsha (rain), Sharad (early autumn), Hemanta (late autumn) and Shishira (winter).

The season of Vasants is centered around the day of spring (Vernal) equinox. Two months leading to the day of the summer solstice constituted the season of Grishma, while two months following the day of the summer solstice constituted the season of Varsha. The season of Sharad centered around the day of the fall (Sharad) equinox. Two months leading to the day of the winter solstice constituted the season of Hemanta while two months following the day of the winter solstice constituted the season Shishira.

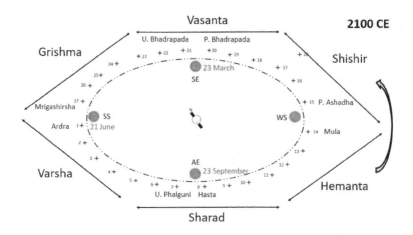

5.5 Precession of the Earth's Axis (Precession of Equinoxes)

The precession of equinoxes is the phenomenon of the move-ment of the earth's axis in a circular path that takes about 26000 years to complete one cycle. As the earth's axis moves through a circular path, it traces a circle in the sky. At any given time, where the earth's axis points to, along this circular path, is called the point of "north celestial pole" (NCP). If a distinct and visible star is close to this point of NCP, it attains the status of a "north pole star" for a time, i.e., until the NCP moves far away from the posi-tion of the star.

The modern European world became aware of this phenome-non of the precession of the earth's axis only very recently (about 2000 years ago) via observations of Egyptians, and since the ob-servations that led to this awareness were based on movement of the point of equinoxes, the phenomenon was mislabeled as the "precession of equinoxes." Unfortunately, the name has stuck and is now widely used in modern astronomy literature.

This phenomenon of the precession of the earth's axis (Ayana) and its corresponding consequences, coupled with the ingenious indian invention of the luni-solar calendar, is responsible for our ability to analyze astronomy and chronology references from an-cient Indian narratives and to determine the chronology of ancient Indian civilization, and by implication, ancient civilizations of the world.

5.5.1 Change in the Location of the North Celestial Pole (NCP)

The precession of the earth's axis results in change of location for the north celestial point (NCP). Thus, a bright star that can act as visible proxy for the NCP would also change with the change in the location of NCP.

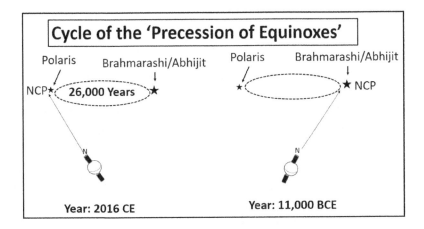

For example, while "Polaris" is the north pole star in our times, Vega (Abhijit/Brahmarashi) was the north pole star around 12000 BCE.

5.5.2 Change in the Position of the Sun

The timing (day, lunar month, and tithi) of the winter solstice would shift with respect to the background reference frame of a nakshatra by about one day (one degree) every 72 years. This means the point of winter solstice would shift by about one nakshatra every one-thousand year (26000 / 27 = 963 ~ 1000).

In our times (21st century, 2100 CE), the position of the sun is between nakshatra Mula and nakshatra Purva Ashaadha on the day of the winter solstice, and it is between nakshatra Ardra and nakshatra Mrigashirsha on the day of the summer solstice (Figure 4).

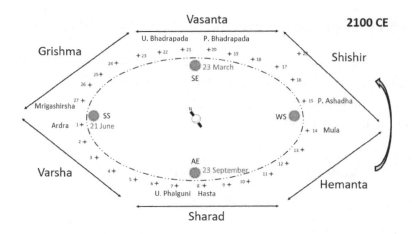

If we go back in antiquity by about 7500 years, the position of the sun for the day of the winter solstice would shift from nakshatra Mula/Purva Ashaadha to nakshatra Uttara Bhadrapada; and the position of the sun for the day of the summer solstice, would shift from nakshatra Ardra/Mrigashirsha to nakshatra Hasta/Uttara Phalguni. A shift of about 7 nakshatras would occur, as expected, corresponding to ~7000 years.

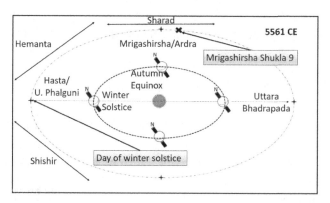

5.5.3 Shift of seasons with respect to the lunar months

The lunar month of Chaitra occurs during the second half of Vasanta ritu (spring) in our times. If we go back, halfway through the cycle of the precession of equinoxes, to ~11000 BCE, the lunar month of Chaitra coincided with the second half of Sharad Ritu (pre-autumn).

The lunar month of Ashwin occurs during the second half of Sharad ritu (pre-autumn) in our times. If we go back, halfway through the cycle of the precession of equinoxes, to ~11000 BCE, the lunar month of Ashwin coincided with the second half of Vasanta ritu (spring). In other words, the points of all cardinal points (solstices & equinoxes) had reversed (2016 CE vs 11000 BCE).

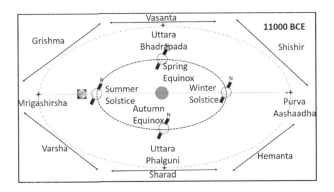

5.6 Julian and Gregorian Calendars

The Julian calendar, a reform of the Roman calendar, was introduced by Julius Caesar in 46 BCE and came into force in 45 BCE. It was designed to approximate the tropical year. It has a regular year of 365 days divided into 12 months, and a leap day added to February, every 4 years which makes the average Julian year 365.25 days long. The Julian calendar overestimates the length of the year by ~0.0078 days and this discrepancy results in the shifting of equinox or solstice days over a long period.

The Gregorian calendar was introduced in 1582 CE. The Gregorian calendar modified the Julian calendar's regular cycle of leap years, years exactly divisible by four, by introducing a caveat – every year that is exactly divisible by four is a leap year, except for years that are exactly divisible by 100; the centurial years that are exactly divisible by 400 are still leap years. Thus, the year 1900 is not a leap year, but the year 2000 is a leap year. This modification changed the mean length of the calendar year from 365.25 days to 365.2425 days. The Gregorian calendar also dealt with the past-accumulated difference between these lengths. The Roman Catholic Church thought that the first council of Nicaea had fixed the vernal equinox on 21 March and by the time of Gregory's edict for the modification of the calendar in 1582 CE, the vernal equinox had moved backwards in the calendar and was occurring on about 11 March, 10 days earlier. The Gregory calendar therefore began by dropping 10 calendar days (5-14 October in 1582 CE), to revert to the previous date of the vernal equinox. The marginal difference of 0.000125 days between the Gregorian calendar average year and the actual year means that, in around 8000 years, the calendar will be about one day behind where it is now. It is important to remember that the earth's rotation also experiences some variation and thus the change in the length of the vernal equinox year cannot be accurately predicted.

Historical research uses the Gregorian calendar for the events after the 16th century and uses the Julian calendar for the events before the 16th century.

5.7 Delta T and Dynamic Time

This is the difference between Universal Time (UTC) and Terrestrial Dynamic Time (TDT). TDT is based on atomic clocks, and it is the standard for precise time keeping in astronomy. It differs from UTC because the earth's rotation is slowing in an irregular manner. This is due to the earth's gravitational interaction with the moon. We must periodically add or subtract "leap seconds" to or from UTC, to keep it in sync with where the earth is pointing. The accumulated difference between UTC and TDT is called "Delta T."

The current value of "Delta T" is about 67 seconds. But in 4000 BCE, the accumulated time correction was about two days, and in much earlier periods, it was only an educated guess. Note that

"Delta T" affects the time when an astronomical event is observed on earth, and hence the altitude and azimuth where it is seen in the sky.

5.8 Caution While Using the Solar Calendar as Reference

The "Julian" calendar experiences the shift of one day every ~128 years in the timing of the day of the winter solstice. For example, it was assumed that the day of the winter solstice occurred, per this Julian calendar, on 21 December during the year 45 BCE. This meant, after 128 years (i.e. ~83 CE) the day of the winter solstice began occurring on 20 December. As one goes in further antiquity, beyond 45 BCE, the day of winter solstice would shift by one day on Julian calendar every ~128 years, but in the other direction. For example, the day of the winter solstice occurred on 31 January in the year 5560 BCE.

The current solar calendar in use is the 'Gregorian' calendar. The usage of this calendar began in 1582 CE. Per this calendar, the day of the winter solstice is fixed at 21 December. This scenario will continue, without significant change, for a foreseeable future.

5.9 What is Central Tithi^{TM}?

I introduce a new concept called 'Central Tithi^{TM}. I have employed this concept at least since 2009 CE; however, I had used other names such as 'median tithi'. 'Central Tithi'is the most appropriate name. 'Median tithi'is not correct and will mislead many, especially those familiar with the definition of "median" from statistics.

To understand the concept of "Central Tithi," it is useful to ask the following question:

> If the day of the winter solstice is fixed at 21 December, per current solar reference calendar (Gregorian), what is the lunar tithi and lunar month for this day of the winter solstice?

We would not be able to easily answer this question. We will

125

require additional information, for example, which specific year (e.g., 1999 CE?) and even then, we will need to perform additional calculations or refer to a Panchang for that specific year to answer the question of lunar tithi and lunar month. In 1999 CE, the tithi for the day of the winter solstice was Margashirsha Shukla 14 (Chaturdashi).

This is because the lunar tithi (and the lunar month) for the day of the winter solstice is not fixed, unlike 21 December of the Gregorian calendar. Recall that there is a gap of about 10-11 days between a lunar year and a solar year, with the lunar year shorter by 10-11 days. This means a lunar tithi would shift by about 10-11 tithis every year for the day of the winter solstice, while the solar day (per solar reference calendar) would remain fixed at 21 December.

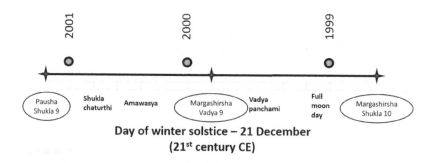

Day of winter solstice – 21 December
(21ˢᵗ century CE)

Of course, this shift would not continue forever. After about 2-3 years, the lunar year would be synchronized with the solar year by the insertion of Adhika masa, which would result in an abrupt change of the tithi for the day of the winter solstice.

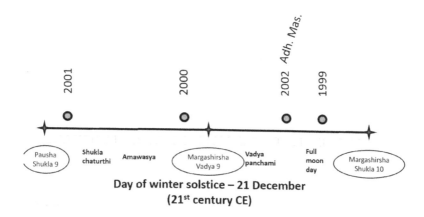

Day of winter solstice – 21 December
(21st century CE)

After this abrupt change, the tithi would shift by about 10-11 days until it is time for another Adhika masa.

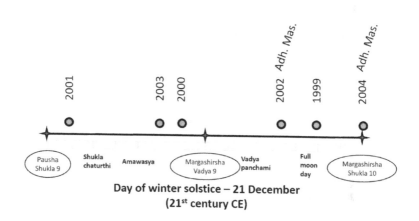

Day of winter solstice – 21 December
(21st century CE)

If we plot lunar tithi(s) for the day of the winter solstice for the last 20 years (1998-2017 CE), they would occur over an interval of Margashirsha shukla 10 through Pausha shukla 9. The broad interval of about a month-long duration (~30 tithis) over which the day of the winter solstice would coincide is centered around the tithi of Margashirsha vadya/krishna Navami (9). Thus, in our times, the **"Central Tithi"** for the day of winter solstice is **Margashirsha vadya/krishna Navami (9)**.

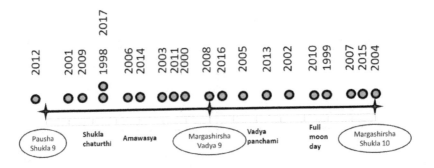

Thus, a "Central Tithi" is the tithi around which the actual tithi(s) for the specific day of cardinal points would occur (+/- 15 tithis).

5.10 Central Tithi and the Precession

Since the point of the winter solstice would move by one degree with respect to the background nakshatra reference frame, due to the precession of the earth's axis every 72 years, the central tithi would also shift by one tithi every 72 years.

5.11 Day of the Winter Solstice

The day of the winter solstice occurs on 21 December, per Gregorian reference calendar in our times. That has been the situation since the Gregorian calendar came into being in 1582 CE. This will continue to be the case for the next 3000 years. The Gregorian calendar uses a peculiar rule for a leap year:

> Every year that is exactly divisible by four is a leap year, except for years that are exactly divisible by 100, but these centurial years are leap years if they are exactly divisible by 400. For example, the years 1700, 1800, and 1900 are not leap years, but the year 2000 is.

The Julian calendar is believed to have begun in 45 BCE. The day of the winter solstice was set at 21 December. Since Julian calendar assumes leap year every 4 years, it ends up shifting the day of winter solstice by one day every ~128 years. This is the

128

reason a correction of about 10 days had accumulated by the time of the institution of Gregorian calendar. It is a convention to use Julian calendar as reference calendar for all events prior to 1582 CE.

For our purposes, it is important to remember that the day of the winter solstice would shift by one day every ~128 years as we go back in antiquity, beginning with 45 BCE (the reference year of the Julian calendar when the day of the winter solstice was set to 21 December). Thus, the day of the winter solstice was on 5 January in 1951 BCE, on 7 January in 2155 BCE, on 8 January in 2448 BCE, on 13 January in 3066 BCE, 14 January in 3142 BCE or 3162 BCE and on 30 January in 5560 BCE.

6

Constraints on the events
of
Bhishma-nirvana

"Problems are hidden opportunities, and constraints can actually boost creativity."
- Martin Villeneuve

We documented all relevant chronology evidence of Bhishma-nirvana and the results of that investigation can be summarized as follows:

(1) Bhishma was on the bed of arrows for more than 92 days. We will use 92 as the lower limit in estimating the constraints related to the events of Bhishma-nirvana. It is important to keep in mind that actual duration is >92.

(2) Bhishma fell in the battle on the 10th day of the war, and since then, he was on the bed of arrows until the day of the winter solstice. The war continued for an additional 8 days.

(3) Yudhishthira and his party spent a month-long interval on the bank of the Ganga river after the war was over and before returning to Hastinapura.

(4) In Hastinapura, Yudhisthira was coronated as the king, and then he went to meet Bhishma. It is on this day that Krishna told Bhishma that Bhishma had 56 more days to live.

(5) Yudhisthira visited Bhishma every day for six consecutive days during which Bhishma advised him on various subjects of Raja-dharma and Moksha-dharma. Bhishma recited "Vishnu-Sahastra-naama" on the sixth and last day

130

and then asked Yudhishtira to return to Hastinapura and only return to him when the sun turned north. (i.e., after the day of the winter solstice).

(6) Yudhishthira returned to Hastinapura and stayed there for 50 nights before returning to Bhishma. Bhishma passed away on that day.

We documented all relevant astronomy evidence of Bhishma-nirvana and the results of the investigation can be summarized as follows:

(1) Most of the 18 days of the Mahabharata war took place during the first part (first month) of the Sharad season.

(2) The Mahabharata war began on the Amavasya day (+/- one day) and ended three to four days after the Purnima day, i.e., the war began and took place during the Shukla paksha (waxing phase) of the lunar month.

(3) The Mahabharata war began on the day of Amavasya and took place during the lunar month of Margashirsha.

(4) The inference of war beginning with Amavasya and thus taking place during the Shukla paksha of the lunar month of Margashirsha is further validated by references to the occurrence of Kartika Purnima and Kartika Krishna Chaturdashi before the beginning of the Mahabharata war.

(5) The inference in (4) is further corroborated by the occurrence of Chaitra Purnima, long after the day of Bhishma-nirvana.

We also introduced the new concept of "Central Tithi" in the chapter on "Astronomy Agama."

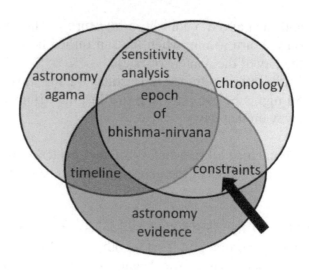

We will combine the chronology and astronomy evidence against the background of astronomy science to establish these constraints using the scientific framework of प्रत्यक्षानुमानागमाः (Samadhipad 7) of sage Patanjali and प्रत्यक्षानुमानोपमानशब्दा (गोतमकृत न्यायदर्शन 1:1:3)) of Gotama. In both cases, the importance of drawing the inference based on objectively testable evidence is emphasized. This can be represented as follows:

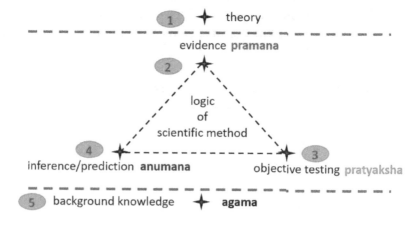

The framework is important for our analysis and we will make ample use of it to illustrate how we arrived at our inferences.

132

CONSTRAINTS

6.1 Constraints on the Timing of the Mahabharata War

We will explore the constraints on the season, lunar paksha (fortnight), and lunar month of the Mahabharata war.

6.1.1 The Season of the Mahabharata War

Bhishma-nirvana occurred on the day (or one day after) of winter solstice and since Bhishma was on the bed of arrows for 92+ days, we can infer that the Mahabharata war itself took place during the first half of Sharad season.

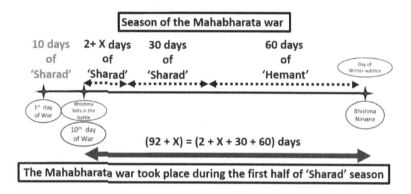

We can explain this inference, using the triad of explanation-prediction-testing as follows:

1. Bhishma-nirvana on the day of winter solstice
2. Bhishma on the bed of arrows for 92+ days
3. Bhishma fell in the battle on the 10th day of the war

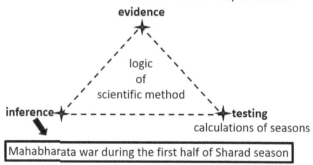

6.1.2 The Lunar Paksha of the Mahabharata War

The Mahabharata text does not refer to the description of the moon during the first seven days of the war. The descriptions of the "full moon-like" moon appear, beginning with the 10th day of the war and continue for two days after the war. The last few days of the war, including two days following the war, are rich in "full moon" descriptions. We can infer via प्रत्यक्षानुमानोपमानशब्दा, that the war began near Amavasya day, and most of it took place during the "Shukla paksha" (waxing phase) of the lunar month.

1. No mention of the moon – first 7 days of the war
2. Rich 'full moon' descriptions – last 7 days of the war

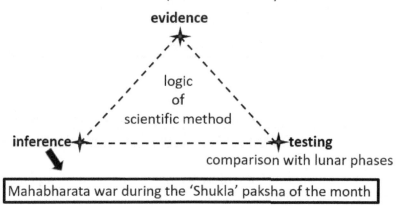

6.1.3 The Lunar Month of the Mahabharata War

The Mahabharata text preserves a few critical references that point to phases and positions of the moon and allow us to identify Margashirsha as the lunar month of the Mahabharata War.

1. 'Full moon like' moon near nakshatra Krittika on the 12ᵗʰ day of war
2. 'Full moon like' moon near nakshatra Punarvasu on the 17ᵗʰ day of war
3. Moon of 'Shukla' paksha rising on the 10ᵗʰ day of the war

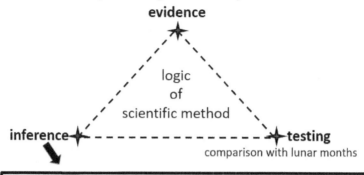

6.2 The Lower Limits on the Tithis of Mahabharata Events

The lower limits of the tithis define the earliest occurrence of the events <u>within the lunar year of the Mahabharata war</u>. We will employ available evidence to determine the lower limits on lunar tithis for the following events:

1. The first day of the Mahabharata war
2. The 10ᵗʰ day of the Mahabharata war when Bhishma fell in the battle
3. The day of Bhishma-nirvana that occurred either on the day of the winter solstice or a day after

6.2.1 The First Day of the Mahabharata War

The Mahabharata text states the occurrence of Kartika full moon and Kartika Krishna Chaturdashi before the war began. Thus, the lower limit of lunar tithi on the first day of the Maha-bharata war is that of **Kartika Amavasya (Kartika Krishna 15)**. This means that the first day of the Mahabharata war <u>cannot be any tithi before the tithi of **Kartika Amawasya**.</u>

135

CONSTRAINTS

6.2.2 The 10th day of the Mahabharata War (Fall of Bhishma)

Once the lower limit on the first day of the Mahabharata war is set, the lower limit on the 10th day of the war is set automatically. We can count 10 tithis from the lower limit for the first day of war and arrive at **Margashirsha Shukla Navami (9)** as the lower limit on the 10th day of the war, when Bhishma fell in the battle and decided to rest on the bed of arrows, until the day of Bhishma-nirvana.

This means that the 10th day of the Mahabharata war <u>cannot be any tithi before the tithi of **Margashirsha Shukla Navami (9)**.</u>

6.2.3 The Day of Bhishma-nirvana

Since we know that Bhishma was on the bed of arrows for more than 92 days, we will employ 92 as the lower limit on his duration on the bed of arrows and then begin counting from the lower limit for the 10th day of the war (Margashirsha Shukla Navami) to arrive at **Phalguna Shukla Dwadashi (12)** as the lower limit for the day of Bhishma-nirvana.

This means that the day of Bhishma-nirvana <u>cannot be any tithi before the tithi of **Phalguna Shukla Dwadashi (12)**</u>.

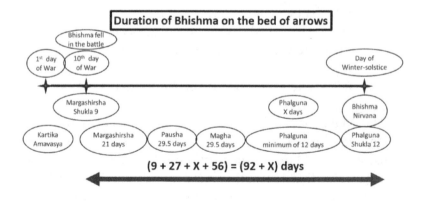

136

6.3 The Upper Limits

The upper limits of the tithis define the latest occurrence of the events within the lunar year of the Mahabharata war.

Since we are going to estimate the upper limits for the identical three events (first and tenth day of the war + day of Bhishma-nirvana), we will explore them in the reverse order.

6.3.1 The Day of Bhishma-nirvana

The Mahabharata text tells us that Bhishma-nirvana occurred long before the day of Chaitra purnima (full moon); however, it does not provide any additional chronological clues. This significant gap between the day of Bhishma-nirvana and Chaitra Purnima can be asserted because sufficient time (whatever that may be) elapsed between these two events; enough for Krishna to visit Dwarka, after the day of Bhishma-nirvana and to return to Hastinapura before Uttara gave birth to Parikshit. The Pandavas were not at Hastinapura when Parikshit was born. The Pandavas returned to Hastinapura with much wealth, and this is when Vyasa suggested initiation of Ashwamedha yajna on the upcoming day of Chaitra Purnima.

Instead of guessing a number for the days between the day of Bhishma-nirvana and Chaitra Purnima, we will employ **Chaitra Purnima** as our upper limit on the tithi of Bhishma-nirvana. Still, it would be useful to keep in mind that Bhishma-nirvana indeed occurred long before the day of Chaitra Purnima.

This means that the day of Bhishma-nirvana cannot be any tithi after the tithi of **Chaitra Purnima (Chaitra Shukla 15)**.

6.3.2 The 10ᵗʰ Day of the War

Things become very interesting and intriguing as we estimate the upper limit for tithi of the 10ᵗʰ day of the war. Beginning with the day of Chaitra purnima and counting backwards by 92 days leads us to the day (tithi) of **Pausha shukla Dwadashi (12)**!

This means that the 10ᵗʰ day of the Mahabharata war cannot be any tithi after the tithi of **Pausha Shukla Dwadashi (12)**.

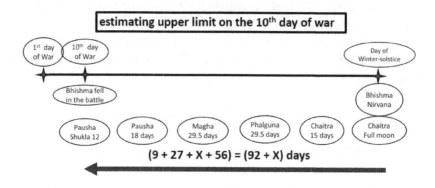

On the other hand, we have two specific constraints for the 10th day of the war:

1. The day must occur during the lunar month of Margashirsha
2. The day must occur during the Shukla paksha of the lunar month

These two constraints demand that the 10th day is further moved back by, first, 12 days (12 days related to the lunar month of Pausha) and then by an additional 15 days for the Krishna paksha of Margashirsha. This movement due to such constraints brings the 10th day of the war within the grasp of "Shukla paksha" of Margashirsha.

On the other hand, enormous evidence based on the phases and positions of the moon of the Mahabharata text asserts that this is not going to be enough to satisfy other constraints. For example - (1). the first day of war cannot be removed from the day of Amavasya by more than one day. (2) the lunar month of the war must be that of Margashirsha or (3) the constraints of having most of the days of the war during the Shukla paksha of Margashirsha.

1. 'Shukla paksha' is the predominant time of the war
2. Margashirsha is the lunar month of the war
3. The first day of war must be Amavasya (+/-1 day)

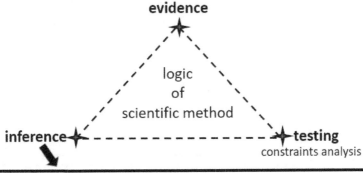

A surprising, intriguing, and impressive conclusion is staring in our face! What is it? The conclusion is that there is no range over which we can determine the tithi for the 10th day of the war! Thus, the upper limit on the 10th day of war is same as its lower limit. The maximum we will able to coax out of these constraints is the ordinary and allowed error of about +/- 1 day due to the variable length of tithis.

The conclusion is that the 10th day of the war, when Bhishma fell in the battle, is fixed at Margashirsha shukla Navami (9).

This means the 10th day of the Mahabharata war cannot be any other tithi but the day of Margashirsha Shukla Navami!

6.3.3 The First Day of the War

The upper limit for the first day of the war is a bygone conclusion. All the restrictions and little error allowed for the 10th day of the war also applies to the first day of the war.

The conclusion is that the first day of the war is fixed at **Kartika Amavasya!**

This means that the first day of the Mahabharata war cannot be any other tithi but the day of Kartika Amavasya (Kartika Krishna 15)!

CONSTRAINTS

1. 'Shukla paksha' is the predominant time of the war
2. Margashirsha is the lunar month of the war
3. The first day of war must be Amavasya (+/-1 day)

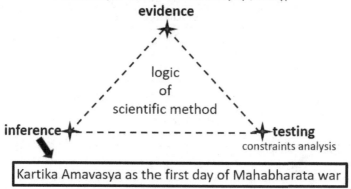

Summary

The first day of the Mahabharata war was the day of Kartika Amavasya (Kartika Krishna 15).

The 10th day of the Mahabharata war was the day of Margashirsha Shukla Navami (9).

The lower limit for the tithi of Bhishma-nirvana is Phalguna shukla 12 and the upper limit for the tithi of Bhishma-nirvana is Chaitra purnima. This means Bhishma-nirvana occurred after Phalguna Shukla Dwadashi (12) and before Chaitra Purnima (Chaitra Shukla 15).

Epoch of Bhishma-nirvana

"Research is of considerable importance in certain fields, such as science and history."
- Fred Saberhagen

We are ready to calculate the mean chronology numbers for the epoch of Bhishma-nirvana. We will do it based on two sets of evidence:

1. Calculations based on the lower and upper limits for the first and 10th day of the war coupled with lower and upper durations for Bhishma on the bed of arrows. This set of evidence provides us with 4700 BCE - 7000 BCE as the interval for the "epoch of Bhishma-nirvana."
2. Calculations based on the lunar month of Margashirsha coinciding with the first half of the Sharad season. This set of evidence provides us with 5642 BCE as the mean year for the chronology of the Mahabharata war, and hence for the "epoch of Bhishma-nirvana."

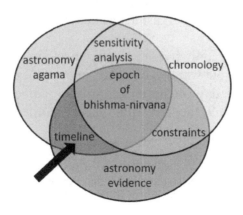

7.1 Lower and Upper Limits

Let's begin with the lower limit for the day of Bhishma-nir-vana. We found out that the Mahabharata evidence provides no flexibility for the tithi of fall of Bhishma (10th day of the war) and it must be virtually fixed at Margashirsha shukla 9 (+/- 1 day). The variability of +/- 1 day is due to error that can occur in determining the tithi of the day due to the varying lengths of tithis (anywhere from 19 hrs to 26 hrs).

It so happens that in our times Margashirsha Shukla Navami (9) is the lower limit of the "tithi range" for the day of the winter solstice.

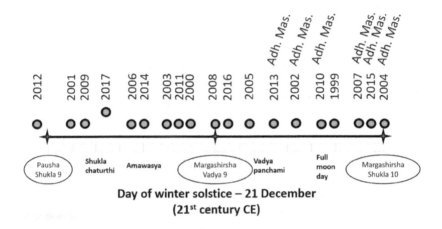

Day of winter solstice – 21 December
(21st century CE)

This means that occasionally, the day of the winter solstice would coincide with Margashirsha shukla 9 in our times, as a limiting case.

Now imagine, only hypothetically-speaking of course, that is, If the Mahabharata war had occurred in our times, in one of those years when the day of the winter solstice coincided with Margashirsha shukla 9, the text would have recorded something like this, ceteris paribus:

> Bhishma fell in the battle on the 10th day of the war. He tilted his head and looked at the sun and noted that the sun had turned north. And thus, this was also the day of Bhishma-nirvana.

In this case, albeit hypothetical, we would have concluded that Bhishma was on the bed of arrows for 0 (zero) days!

On the other hand, the Mahabharata text preserves for us a detailed chronological record that states that Bhishma was on the bed of arrows for more than 92 days. This means we must go backward in time, beginning with our times, for a duration long enough, so that the tithi shifts by at least 92 days. We do know that the "central tithi" shifts by one day every 72 years.

The calculations are rather straightforward. Beginning with our times, and to achieve a shift of 92 tithis (Margashirsha Shukla 9 to Phalguna Shukla 12) would mean we must go backwards by 92 x 72 = 6624 years before present and subtracting ~2000 years of common era (CE) leads us to ~4700 BCE as the lower limit on the "epoch of Bhishma-nirvana."

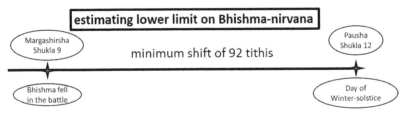

92 (minimum shift) x 72 (years for shift of one tithi) = 6624 years ago

6624 years ago ~ (6624 -2000) ~ **4700 BCE**

We estimate the upper limit on the "epoch of Bhishma-nirvana" by beginning with our times and going backwards to achieve a shift of 125 tithis (Margashirsha Shukla 9 to Chaitra purnima (Chaira shukla 15) and this would mean we must go backwards by 125 x 72 = 9000 before present and subtracting ~2000 years of common erra (CE) leads us to ~7000 BCE as the upper limit on the "epoch of Bhishma-nirvana."

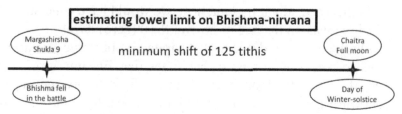

92 (minimum shift) x 72 (years for shift of one tithi) = 6624 years ago

6624 years ago ~ (6624 -2000) ~ **4700 BCE**

7.2 Margashirsha During the First Half of Sharad Season

The Mahabharata text evidence established that the war began near Kartika Amavasya, and most of it took place during the Shukla paksha of Margashirsha and it occurred during the first half of Sharad season. This evidence allows us to estimate the timing of the Mahabharata war and hence that of Bhishma-nirvana.

In our times, the end of Hemanta season and the beginning of Shishir season occurs during the lunar month of Margashirsha. We must go backwards in time until the lunar month of Margashirsha coincides with the first half of Sharad season.

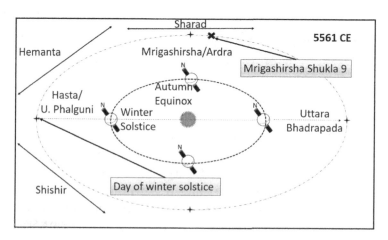

The yogatara of naskahtra Mrigashirsha (Bellatrix) coincided

with the point of the spring equinox around 4460 BCE. This refers to the time of the lunar month of Margashirsha coinciding with the fall equinox (opposite of spring equinox). We must go further backwards in antiquity until the yogatara of nakshatra Mrigashirsha was separated by 15 degrees from the point of spring equinox. This time, when the lunar month of Margashirsha coincided with the first half of Sharad season, can be calculated to be equal to 5642 BCE.

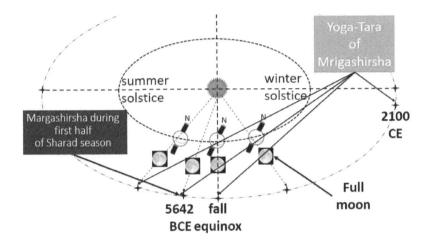

I have already shown in my previous works why 5561 BCE is the year of the Mahabharata war. The mean value calculation estimated a mean year of 5642 BCE which is within less than 100 years from the established 5561 BCE as the year of the Mahabharata war. This is indeed impressive and pleasing.

Thus, 5642 BCE is estimated to be the mean year for the "epoch of the Mahabharata war," and thus for the "epoch of Bhishma-nirvana."

Summary

The first set of evidence, based on upper and lower limits for the first day of Mahabharata war and the day of Bhishma-nirvana, led to an interval of 7000 BCE - 4700 BCE for the "epoch of Bhishma-nirvana."

The second set of evidence, based on the war beginning with Kartika Amavasya, most of it taking place during the Shukla paksha of Margashirsha and during the first half of the Sharad season, led to a mean value of 5642 BCE as the year for the "epoch of the Mahabharata war," and thus for the "epoch of Bhishma-nirvana."

Sensitivity Analysis

"I find intelligence sexy. I find a sense of humor sexy. I find sensitivity sexy."
-   Nicole Appleton

In this chapter, we will test the two results obtained for the "epoch of the Mahabharata war" and/or "the epoch of Bhishma-nirvana" for their robustness by exposing them to various known sources of errors, most of them due to fundamental aspects of astronomy. We will begin with enumeration of these fundamentals of astronomy and the kind of variations to be expected on the "epoch of Bhishma-nirvana" due to their effects.

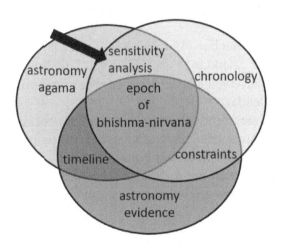

8.1 Potential Sources of Astronomy Errors

In the astronomy world, everything is in motion. Nothing is stationary. It is then amazing and surprising that the evidence that can be analyzed and interpreted with the background knowledge of astronomy can be so decisive.

This has become possible because of the long cycles of astronomy relative to the timelines of human history, and even though everything is moving, we can employ this discipline of science to know more of our past. In fact, our ability to trace specific events of the past and their chronology is very much due to some of these changes of astronomy world.

These movements of astral objects also introduce certain uncertainties, sources of errors and these can lead to variations in our computed results.

Is there a way to estimate the potential impact of these uncertainties on our computed results? There certainly is. However, before we can reassess our computations, we need to understand the effects due to each source of error, the magnitude of these errors, and whether the effect is going to be 'materially significant.'

We will begin with a description of error source and then analyze its impact for our computed results.

8.1.1. Luni-Solar Calendar

The lunar calendar (354 days) is shorter by about 10-11 days than the solar calendar (365-366 days). This leads to a change in the tithi (lunar calendar) for a specific cardinal point (designated via solar calendar).

This change of the tithi within a range for the day of a specific cardinal point is best understood with my concept of 'central tithi'. Thus, corrections via comprehension of "central tithi" is the best way to account for this gap between lunar and solar calendars. No separate correction is required due to the luni-solar calendar.

8.1.2 Adhika Masa

Insertion of an Adhika masa (intercalary month) on an average about every 2.5 years is how the lunar calendar is synchronized with the solar calendar.

148

Adhika masa does have effect on the nomenclature of lunar months, i.e., how a specific interval of about 30 days is named in the lunar calendar. This can lead to a variation or an error in the naming of a lunar month by +/- one month. For example, at times, even when the position of the full moon is near nakshatra Margashirsha, the lunar month might be named as "Pausha."

The key takeaway of this effect is to comprehend that one should analyze ancient references with this plausible variation of +/- 1 lunar month. It may influence how a lunar month is named while an observation is recorded. It does not influence computed results.

8.1.3 Kshaya Masa

Kshaya masa may add to the confusion of the naming of lunar months, not unlike "Adhika masa." However, it is best to ignore visualizing the effect due to "Kshaya masa." The subject is of academic interest, but not relevant to the subject matter discussed in this book.

8.1.4 Error in Tithi Estimation

While the length of a solar day is about 24 hours, the length of lunar tithi (time taken by the moon to travel through its path by 12 degrees, as measured from the earth) varies from about 19 hours to 26 hours. A typical method (variations may exist) is to note down the tithi at the time of sunrise. Depending on when a tithi begins, we may have the same tithi for two consecutive days or a lapse of one tithi at other times.

This introduces an error of about +/- one day in our estimation/designation of a tithi for a given day. Over a period of one complete revolution of the moon around the earth (or within few revolutions), the effect of this variation is cancelled out. Of course, new instances of such variations begin.

All in all, it is sufficient to remember that any specified tithi has an inbuilt error of +/- 1 day due to reasons mentioned, when coupled with its determination by visual means, e.g., a visual observer noting down the phase and position of the moon to determine the tithi.

8.1.5 Proper Motions of Yogatara

All astral objects have their motion, with respect to the background astral field, as seen from the earth. Most of the Yogataras (for corresponding nakshatra) are selected based on their brightness, proximity to the ecliptic, and their stability related to proper motions. This selection of Yogataras has been impressive and has allowed us much investigation of the past.

However, as we go back, in deep antiquity, the effect due to proper motions of Yogatara can affect our calculations. On the other hand, it is also critical to recognize that this same effect can tell us more of our past, too.

It is hard to predict without the context, if a proper motion of a given star/Yogatara will have a significant effect on the specific computation.

All we can say is that in the context of the current subject of Bhishma-nirvana, the effects due to proper motions of Yogatara are of no material consequence.

8.1.6 Expected Variations Around the Central Tithi

The expected variation around "Central Tithi" is +/- 15 days. This amounts to an error of 72 x 15 = 1080 years, i.e., +/- 1080 ~ 1000 years. It is important to remember that this error of +/- 1000 accounts for the error/variation due to multiple sources of variation (luni-solar calendar, adhik masa, kshaya masa, and error in estimation of tithi) discussed so far. Thus, one must be careful not to correct for these multiple sources of variation discussed, in an additive fashion.

For these reasons, I find my concept of "central tithi" useful in accounting for these errors as a one stop solution!

8.1.7 Nonequal Separation Between Yogatara(s)

While mathematically we can divide the astral sphere or ecliptic into 360 degrees, we do not have this luxury to place our stars (astral markers to track positions of astral objects or astral phenomenon) in the sky as desired. In addition, the proper motions of these astral objects coupled with astral phenomenon such as the precession of the earth's axis would dismantle whatever design we come up with in no time.

Nonequal separation of Yogataras or other astral objects is not the only issue when it comes to calendrical computations (e.g., nomenclature of lunar months). Hard-to-predict movements of the moon coupled with definitions for the designation of lunar months, based on the positions of the moon over a wide area of the sky leads to much confusion in the designation of a specific lunar month, in addition to the effects, already discussed due to the insertion of an adhika masa.

The way to deal with these imperfections is to make calculations based on the positions of Yogatara or relevant astral objects and carry out alternate calculations based on an ideal division of the sky (sphere, ecliptic, etc.) into equal portions. These two sets of calculations can be assessed to determine if the effect due to positions of "Yogatara" is of material significance. Otherwise, the unnecessary and illogical demand of pretentious precision can only lead to confusion.

8.1.8 Movement of the Moon

The movement of the moon is most difficult to predict. This has many consequences; however, the most relevant for our subject of "Bhishma-nirvana" is how a specific interval (of time) is designated in the language of Indian "lunar months."

"Central Tithi" corrections would take care of the estimation of error in our computed results. However, it is not capable of eliminating the errors in how a given individual would have designated a lunar month at any given time.

These errors of designating a specific interval as referring to a specific month (e.g., Margashirsha, Pausha, Magha, Phalguna, Chaitra, Vaishakha, etc.) occur in our times (they occur regularly in the Panchanga and are not even considered errors), and we should expect the same for ancient times.

I am asked this question all the time. What is the cause of this real or apparent confusion in the designation of lunar months seen in our modern Panchanga or researchers discussing forever the confusion of lunar months and tithis from ancient Indian narratives? It is better to start answering such questions by stating that we truly don't know. Having said that, the situation is not as desperate as it may seem. We can pin-point specific reasons as to what causes this confusion in our times and what might have led to similar confusion in ancient times. We can also specify what cautions to exercise in researching ancient Indian narratives via archeo-astronomy.

While there are 27 (or 28) nakshatras, there are only 12 lunar months. And while there are only 12 solar months, an additional lunar month needs to be inserted at a periodic interval (about every 2.5 years) to bring the lunar calendar in sync with that of the solar calendar. And while a rule exists for determining the designation of an interval as a specific lunar month by noting down (or by mathematical calculations) the proximity of the position of the full moon with respect to the background nakshatra reference frame, it is important to realize that these rules are designed to take into account the reality of the hard-to-predict movement of the moon, the reality of the gap between lunar and solar calendar, the reality of the awkward number of nakshatras attributed to an interval of one lunar (or solar) month and finally, the slow but continuous movement of the background nakshatra and astral reference frame cased by the phenomenon of the precession of the earth's axis. So, what gives?

What this means is that while lunar months and lunar tithis are of utmost importance in archeo-astronomy investigations of ancient Indian narratives, they should be recognized for what they are - effects due to near-earth phenomeon. This means, the discussion of lunar tithis and lunar months can only occur after one has determined the plausible interval via other means, specifically via evidence related to long-term phenomenon such as precession of the earth's axis or the cycle of the earth's obliquity.

8.2 Sensitivity Analysis for Interval 7000 BCE - 4700 BCE

The beauty of the concept of "Central Tithi" is such that we will able to perform our sensitivity analysis using this single concept and by assigning errors estimated due to this single concept.

Recall that we estimated the lower limit of 4700 BCE by beginning with Margashirsha Shukla 9 as the day when Bhishma fell in the battle and then counting for 92 days (~94 tithis) to Phalguna Shukla 12. We know that there is a variation of up to +/- 15 days associated with tithis matching a specific cardinal point (in this case, the day of the winter solstice).

We can account for this plausible error by defining our lower limit as 4700 BCE +/- 1080 years or 3700 BCE through 5700 BCE. What is important is to note down the newly arrived lower limit of 3700 BCE, based on this sensitivity analysis.

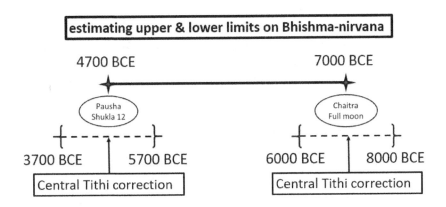

Recall that the calculations leading to 3700 BCE as the lowest limit for the epoch of Bhishma-nirvana is based on the most conservative assumptions made every step of the way, and thus we can say with great conviction that the "epoch of Bhishma-nirvana," and hence the chronology of the Mahabharata war, cannot be later (even a day or year) than 3700 BCE.

This falsifies practically all alternate claims for the chronology of the Mahabharata war.

Similar analysis on the upper limit of 7000 BCE would lead us to the uppermost limit of 8000 BCE for the "epoch of Bhishma-nirvana." It is important to realize that we are doing these sensitivity calculations to test the robustness of our conclusions. We are not saying that the Mahabharata war or Bhishma-nirvana occurred anywhere close to 3700 BCE or 8000 BCE. Rather, the point of emphasis that is worth comprehending is that these events did not happen any time after 3700 BCE or before 8000 BCE.

8.3 Sensitivity Analysis for Mean Year of 5642 BCE

The mean year of 5642 BCE, when the lunar month of Margashirsha coincided with the first half of Sharad season, was calculated by aligning the position of Yogatara of the nakshatra Mrigashirsha corresponding to this location for the first part of Sharad season.

The sensitivity analysis for this mean value can be performed rather easily, with the help of "Central Tithi." The central tithi inherent in the calculations of mean year of 5642 BCE is that of Margashirsha purnima (Shukla 15). The Lunar month of Margashirsha would have continued to be the first month of Sharad season over a period of 5642 BCE +/- 1080 years, i.e., 4562 BCE – 6722 BCE.

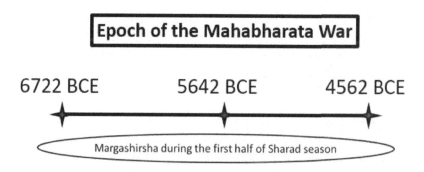

Again, the point of emphasis worth comprehending is that the Mahabharata war occurred sometime between 4562 BCE and 6722 BCE.

If we add the assertion of the Mahabharata text that the war began on Kartika Amavasya and that most of it took place during the Shukla paksha of Margashirsha, then we can further refine the mean year from 5642 BCE to 6205 BCE, i.e., by centering the Shukla paskha of Margashirsha around the first half of Sharad season.

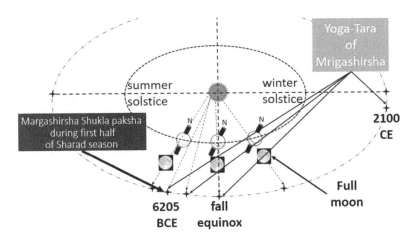

This would mean the Mahabharata war occurred sometime before 5125 BCE and after 7285 BCE.

Epoch of the Mahabharata War (refined)

7285 BCE   6205 BCE   5125 BCE

Margashirsha Shukla Paksha
during
the first half of Sharad season

Summary

Sensitivity analysis allows us to check the robustness of our conclusions. We did just that for the inference arrived via two specific sets of evidence.

Based on the evidence and the corresponding sensitivity analysis of the lower and upper limits for the day of Bhishma-nirvana, the epoch of Bhishma-nirvana and the Mahabharata war happened some time before 3700 BCE and after 8000 BCE.

Based on the evidence and the corresponding sensitivity analysis of Margashirsha as the lunar month of the war and that it occurred during the first half of Sharad season, the epoch of Bhishma-nirvana and the Mahabharata war happened some time before 4562 BCE and after 6722 BCE.

Based on the evidence and the corresponding sensitivity analysis of the war beginning with Kartika Amavasya, occuring during Shukla paksha of Margashirsha and the month of Margashirsha during the first half of Sharad season, the epoch of Bhishma-nirvana and the Mahabharata war happened some time before 5125 BCE and after 7285 BCE.

The combined outcome of sensitivity analysis produced a crisp interval of ~1600 years (5125 BCE – 6722 BCE) for the epoch of Bhishma-nirvana and the Mahabharata war.

Truthlikeness

"Measure what is measurable and make measurable what is not so."

    - Galileo Galilei

9.1 Science and Theories

In a scientific world, multiple theories exist as plausible solutions to a specific problem. In most cases, it is not difficult to determine which among those multiple theories is the best theory at any given point in time. This is because the empirical observations and results are not debated.

On the other hand, in case of history research, the textual evidence can have multiple interpretations. In addition, researchers proposing new theories may assume drastically different fundamental suppositions (e.g., astronomy vs. astrology) or diametrically opposite views (e.g., planets vs. comets).

To overcome this challenge of objective comparison between two theories, the efficacy of a theory is tested by measuring its ability to explain the phenomenon it was conceived to explain. This efficacy can be quantified. The theory must achieve this without compromising its own consistency.

The efficacy of a theory is also assessed via the following qualitative criteria:

1. Ability of the theory to explain a phenomenon not explained previously by other theories
2. Ability of the theory to preserve the successes of previous theories
3. Ability of the theory in making new predictions not made

by previous theories and/or not possible due to previous theories

4. The new predictions, so made, by the theory come to fruition, i.e., they come out true

5. Ability of the theory to lead to growth of knowledge via new predictions and inferences of the theory, suggestions of new experiments, generation of new problems of higher complexity and overall growth of knowledge. The last criteria of "overall growth of knowledge" is vague; however, it is still listed to include anything that is missed by these five points.

9.2 Truthlikeness Score

Let's focus on the "quantitative criteria" of the theory. The criterion was suggested by Sir Karl Popper and is called either 'Truthlikeness' score or 'Verisimilitude' score. We will stick to the use of 'Truthlikeness score' (TS). Truthlikeness Score (TS) reveals the quantitative strength of the theory/claim without wishing away any observations that might conflict with the assertion.

A Truthlikeness score of a theory can be defined as:

Truthlikeness Score (TS) =

(Number of observations corroborated by the theory)
– (minus)
(Number of observations not-corroborated by the theory)

9.3 Physical and Historical Sciences

Let's return to the world of ancient history and chronology research. In science, a theory proposed to solve the identical problem must evaluate all the relevant data/evidence, objectively test all data/evidence, and then compute the Truthlikeness score. This is also required of a theory proposed to solve the problem of chronology of ancient events. Unfortunately, the majority of history researchers are ignorant of this requirement.

For example, about 60 Mahabharata researchers and about 12 Ramayana researchers have proposed 'astronomy' theory to claim chronology of these ancient events. On the other hand, almost all researchers have selected only arbitrary, or, selective sets of data to test their theories. We can show that all of them, chose, a different set of data, in a selective manner, to find corroboration for their claimed chronology. We can also show that the data/evidence avoided, deliberately or ignorantly, by these researchers would have falsified their claims instantaneously. Against this background, I wondered if it was possible to develop a method to critique individual theories/claims and compare them amongst each other.

9.4 Truthlikeness Method™

The Truthlikeness method™ combines the quantitative measurement of the Truthlikeness score (TS) with the qualitative assessment of a theory/claim into a combined report.

9.4.1 All Relevant Evidence

All the principles and logic of physical theories apply to theories for determining the chronology of ancient events. The specific point we had to insist for historical theories/claims was that of the inclusion of all relevant evidence. Since there are more than 100 theories and corresponding claims based on selective evidence, it is of paramount importance that each of these theories/claims should be tested against a maximum number of data/evidence/observations, irrespective of if a specific researcher has tested the specific data/evidence/observation or not.

9.4.2 Consistency of a Theory

In the field of physical sciences, a gap between evidence and ability of a theory to explain all evidence/observations is considered acceptable, on the other hand, a contradiction or inconsistency of a theory in explaining the evidence would immediately lead to dismissal of a theory. The demand on theories for chronology of ancient events should have been no different. Unfortunately, the rot of illogical methods, combining of dogma with testable evidence, blatant ignorance of evidence that would falsify a theory instantaneously, lack of awareness of the need to expose one's theory to severe tests, and to welcome open criticism by fellow researchers is alien to the majority of researchers in this field of ancient chronology research. Education of these researchers on the basic methods and logic of scientific discovery would take time. Since the majority of the theories and the corresponding claims would fall like a house of cards, we should expect severe resistance from these researchers. It is hoped that both producers and consumers of such research comprehend the seriousness of the issue and act quickly.

9.4.3 Introduction of 'Auxiliary' Hypotheses

The next problem is that of researchers employing 'auxiliary theories/hypotheses.' The introduction of "auxiliary" theories by itself is not a bad thing. A good number of inventions and new insights to existing theories in science have occurred due to such 'auxiliary' theories. However, what we must insist is that 'auxiliary' theories should lead to testing of so-far-untested observations and not lead to "explaining away" of such observations. Thus, the introduction of a new 'auxiliary' hypothesis should lead to either additional testing of already-identified evidence and/or identification of new evidence in the light of this new 'auxiliary' hypothesis.

9.4.4 Falsification of Theories and Claims

The next issue we need to address is that of evidence and testing of which leads to the falsification of numerous claims. The majority of researchers of ancient chronology are simply illiterate when it comes to inferential acumen and fail to comprehend falsification of their claims by decisive evidence such as AV observation or evidence of Bhishma-nirvana presented in this book. We can address this issue by simply listing the number of instances the theory/claim has been falsified.

9.4.5 Nontestable Evidence

It is not unusual to run into the evidence that passes the test of relevance with respect to the theory proposed (e.g., astronomy theory of visual observations). On the other hand, the description of the evidence may not lead to clear interpretation and thus may lead to nontestability. The problem becomes worse when a piece of evidence can be tested in the light of one theory but leads to nontestability in the light of another theory. We can address the issue by listing instances of nontestability irrespective of whether another researcher/theory succeeded in testing such an evidence or not.

9.4.6 Qualitative Assessment

A qualitative assessment of a theory based on the five-point criteria outlined in section 9.1 should also be part of the overall assessment of a theory.

9.4.7 Truthlikeness Score

Insistance on the usage of the Truthlikeness Score (TS) leads to the transformation of evidence from the world of metaphysics (views, opinions, and agreements) to the world of objective testing. This also leads to transition from the illogical method of arbitrary or selective evidence usage to the logical method of using all relevant evidence.

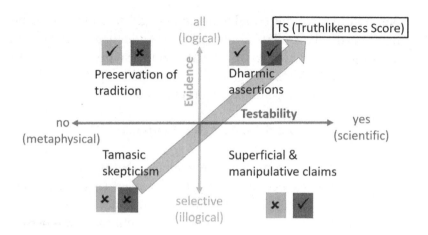

The scientific method insists on the inclusion of all relevant data/evidence in calculating the Truthlikeness Score. In addition, it also important to recognize the hierarchy of evidence, auxiliary hypotheses, background assumptions, and inferences. This hierarchy for a specific theory/claim can be defined with the help of a few basic rules:

1. Only those things (background assumptions, evidence, ad hoc hypotheses, etc.) that lead to an inference are below the hierarchy of that inference
2. Eliminate all ad hoc hypotheses that do not contribute to the testing and outcome of the theory/claim
3. The Truthlikeness Score can be calculated at any stage of hierarchy. The overall Truthlikeness Score is the cumulative Truthlikeness Score of previous stages in hierarchy
4. No double-counting of evidence if the same evidence has contributed multiple times to stages in hierarchy above or in parallel
5. No points for background assumptions employed
6. No points for introduction of "ad hoc" hypotheses
7. The TS hierarchy should be mapped top-down.
8. The calculations of TS score should be done bottoms-up while ensuring no double-counting of evidence takes place.

162

An illustration of this hierarchy of Truthlikeness Score for the case of my theory and claim (Mahabharta war) is presented below:

Hierarchy level 1

Hierarchy level 1 shows the TS top-down diagram for the assertion of 5561 BCE as the year of the Mahabharata war. This is a demonstration of rules 1 and 7.

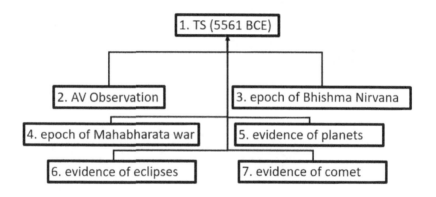

Hierarchy level 2

The next diagram is at Hierarchy level 2. This diagram demonstrates rules 1, 3, 5, and 8. The overall TS score of (57-2) is the cumulative score of previous stages in the hierarchy. No points were assigned to "precession of earth's axis," since it is the background assumption. The calculations of the TS score were done bottom-top.

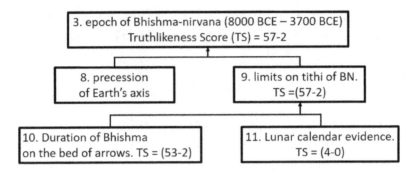

The next diagram (also at Hierarchy level 2) demonstrates rule 4. The evidence that led to assertions 13 and 14 is identical and thus no TS score is shown for assertion 14. This is to ensure that no double-counting of evidence takes place. The diagram also demonstrates rules 1, 3, 5, and 8.

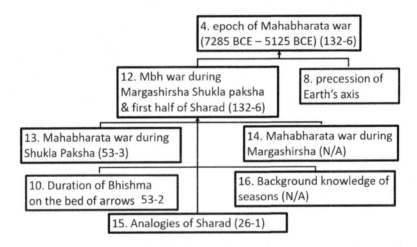

When TS scores from two diagrams above (Hierarchy level 2) are combined to the Hierarchy level 1, care should be taken to ensure that no double-counting of scores due to assertion 10 occurs. For example, we may keep the score of assertion 4 as is (132-6) and modify score of assertion 3 (57-2) to (4-0). This means a combined score of assertions 3 and 4 that would contribute to Hierarchy level 1 would be (136-6).

9.4.8 TS Template™

Truthlikeness score Template (TS Template™) allows objective comparison of each claim with multiple alternate claims using identical criteria.

Comparison between claims, before the evidence is evaluated is shown in this TS Template – before evaluation™.

Researcher		Nilesh Oak	Narahari Achar	R N Iyengar	Saroj Bala	Ashok Bhatnagar	Mohan Gupta	Vedveer Arya
Criterion	Desired							
Year Proposed	N/A	5561 BCE	3067 BCE	1478 BCE	3139 BCE *	1793 BCE *	1952 BCE	3163 BCE
Sticking to one discipline of science?	Yes	Yes	No	No	No	No	No	No
Clear Statement of a theory?	Yes	Yes	No	No	No	No	No	No
All evidence listed?	Yes	Yes	No	No	No	No	No	No
Theory leads to objective testing?	Yes	Yes	No	No	No	No	No	No
Auxiliary hypotheses?	N/A	No	Yes	Yes	No	Yes	Yes	Yes
Consistency of a theory?	Yes	Yes	No	No	No	No	No	No

This is a simple illustration of the Truthlikeness Method™ and how it can be applied to the research of ancient Indian history.

Comparison of multiple claims, after the evidence is evaluated, is shown in this TS Template – after evaluation™. This evaluation would consider six specific criteria (as suggested by Sir Karl Popper) between two theories/claims T/C_1 and T/C_2.

1. T/C_2 makes more precise assertions than T/C_1, and these more precise assertions stand up to more precise tests.
2. T/C_2 takes account of, and explains, more facts than T/C_1.
3. T/C_2 describes, or explains, the facts in more detail than T/C_1.
4. T/C_2 has passed tests which T/C_1 had failed to pass.
5. T/C_2 has suggested new experimental tests, not considered before T/C_2 was designed (and not suggested by T/C_1, and perhaps not even applicable to T/C_1); and T/C_2 has passed these tests.

165

6. T/C_2 has unified or connected various unrelated problems not addressed by all existing/previous theories and claims.

TS (Truthlikeness Score) combines the idea of truth and of content into one measurable number.

It goes without saying that my theory of 'visual observations of the sky' and the claim of 5561 BCE as the year of Mahabharata war scores high on all six criteria of comparison between any two theories and on Truthlikenss score (210-5).

Thus, while there are 130+ competitors for the year of Mahabharata war, when it comes to 5561 BCE, there is no competition!

Criterion	Desired outcome	Nilesh Oak	Narahari Achar	R N Iyengar	Saroj Bala	Ashok Bhatnagar	Mohan Gupta	Vedveer Arya
Year Proposed	N/A	5561 BCE	3067 BCE	1478 BCE	3139 BCE *	1793 BCE *	1952 BCE	3163 BCE
Falsified?	No	No	Yes	Yes	Yes	Yes	Yes	Yes
Non-testable obs?	No	Yes	Yes	Yes	Yes	Yes	Yes	Yes
Theory/claim explains new evidence?	Yes	Yes	No	No	No	No	No	No
Preserves past unrefuted evidence?	Yes	Yes	No	No	No	No	No	No
Theory/claim leads to new predictions?	Yes	Yes	No	No	No	No	No	No
Validation of new predictions?	Yes	Yes	No	No	No	No	No	No
TS Score (C-True - C-False)	High-Low	210-5	1-214	0-215	10-205*	2-213*	3-212	Don't know
Positive TS Score	Yes	Yes	No	No	No	No	No	Don't know
TS Score better than other claims?	Yes	Yes	No	No	No	No	No	Don't know

10

Conflicting Observations

"There must be no barriers to freedom of inquiry. There is no place for dogma in science. The scientist is free, and must be free to ask any question, to doubt any assertion, to seek for any evidence, to correct any errors."
- J. Robert Oppenheimer

Ancient narrations contain observations that contradict each other, within a specific text or between specific texts. The Mahabharata text is not an exception to this reality. The majority of Mahabharata researchers are intimidated by such conflicting evidence and they approach this problem by denying it, hiding under it, and hoping that no one notices.

Of course, what can be considered conflicting evidence depends on how one arrived at his. Instead of listing all relevant evidence that corroborates and conflicts for one's claim, these researchers discuss only that evidence that tends to support their claims. These researchers avoid, ignore, and deny all evidence that would either conflict, or worse, falsify their claim. They undermine such evidence and/or explain it away when caught red-handed and when they realize that avoiding, ignoring, or denying is not an option. This illogical approach naturally leads to erroneous results. But even when, by luck, such illogical methods lead to a correct result, the critical analysis and comparison of multiple claims remains a challenge.

The Truthlikeness Method™ provides a solution to the challenge of enabling comparison of multiple claims.

We do not have to stop by simply listing observations that conflict with our claim. There is much more that one can do with these apparent or real conflicting observations for one's claim. They can be critically discussed and analyzed, and by luck, one

167

may succeed in explaining them (not explaining them away). In some cases, it is possible, as I have shown in my previous books, to demonstrate the interpolated nature of such observations and to show what might have led to such interpolations. It is also possible to demonstrate, as I have also shown in my previous books, how combinations of errors (translation, transcription, transliteration, transposition, interpolation, etc.) can lead to formation of conflicting evidence.

Let's analyze six specific instances of evidence/observations that appear to conflict with my claims for the details of Bhishma-nirvana.

10.1 Bhishma on the Bed of Arrows for Only 58 Days

Most Mahabharata researchers believe in this dogma of Bhishma lying on the bed of arrows for only 58 days. This dogma is so entrenched in the popular psyche that Mahabharata researchers and enthusiasts take this for granted. Since numerous researchers were referring to it, I, too, assumed that the duration of 58 days much be the correct number. I assumed, naively but justifiably, that these researchers must have read the Mahabharata text. I was wrong.

When I decided to determine the chronology of the Mahabharata war, each piece of evidence led me to the year 5561 BCE r. The claim for 5561 BCE as the year of the Mahabharata war is not my original claim. This is because Dr. P. V. Vartak had proposed this year based on different methodology that combined gut feel/intuition with evidence of the Mahabharata text along with evidence of Puranas and the rest of the ancient Indian narratives. Naturally, when I began researching the events of Bhishma-nirvana, still in the context of my first book, I wanted to find out what Dr. Vartak had proposed for the day of Bhishma-nirvana.

Dr. Vartak had assumed the duration of Bhishma on the bed of arrows to be equal to 58 days. However, he collected almost all relevant references of Bhishma-nirvana and realized that they were conflicting with the claim of 58 days. He made multiple attempts to interpret and re-interpret, rationalize, and justify his interpretations to make the case for 58 days for Bhishma on the bed of arrows. The details of his attempts can be read in his book "Swayambhu" (originally in Marathi; however, an English translation is available) or in my first book, 'When did the Mahabharata war happen? The Mystery of Arundhati'.

The takeaway for our current discussion is that I also began with this assumption of 58 days. However, as I went deep into my investigation, I realized that this assumption/claim of 58 days was untenable. Even then, and not unlike Dr. Vartak, I spent about 6 months trying to interprete and to re-interprete, proposing "ad hoc" hypotheses to rationalize and to justify the assumption of 58 days.

Here was my dilemma; I had tested the claim of 5561 BCE for the year and the claim of 16 October for the first day of the Mahabharata war with great success and the claim was supported by enormous evidence. On the other hand, the duration for Bhishma on the bed of arrows, calculated from the 10th day of the war (25 October 5561 BCE) until the day of the winter solstice (31 October 5560 BCE), amounted to 98 days. This duration of 98 days could not be reconciled with the claim of 58 days. I wrote:

> I felt as if I had reached a dead end. *The difference of more than 1-2 days was unacceptable*; never mind the difference of 40 days! I decided to accept the conclusion that the year 5561 BCE, although superior to any other attempt and despite being the best approximation to the truth, was at least not corroborated by the Mahabharata observations related to *Bhishma Nirvana*. (*emphasis mine*)

I wondered what led other researchers to feel cocksure about their assumption of 58 days and if they were successful in corroborating this evidence for their claimed year of the Mahabharata war. I did analyze works of other researchers, and what I discovered can only be described as a "royal disaster." I wrote:

> Naturally, I was curious to verify corroboration claimed by other researchers for the day of *Bhishma Nirvana*. Other researchers have proposed multiple years separated by millenniums. These researchers were not only convinced that they could explain the Mahabharata observations of *Bhishma Nirvana* but also considered these Mahabharata

observations as critical in building their timeline. What is more interesting is the fact that these researchers were blissfully unaware of the contradictions their proposed day of *Bhishma Nirvana* posed for these observations.

In the next chapter, we will look at some of the illogical attempts of researchers trying to rationalize and justify the duration of 58 days for Bhishma on the bed of arrows.

Let's return to my dilemma of 98 days vs. 58 days. My Shraddha and Nishtha in the words of Vyasa was being tested. As a last resort, before giving up, I decided to try an ingenious experiment:

> I speculated, purely from the idea of truth, i.e. if my theory, and its predictions were independently testable, was also true, my theory would then provide me with successful predictions, and I should be able to find observations corroborating my proposed timeline.

And what was my action plan?

> I decided to re-read the Mahabharata text, this time, with emphasis on post-war incidents. I re-read the Mahabharata text, by now a familiar and useful exercise, specifically Bhishma and Shalya and then Sauptic, Stri, Shanti and Anushasan *Parvas*, looking for all observations that would allow me to build the timeline between "Fall of Bhishma" and "*Bhishma Nirvana*". I was, by luck, immensely rewarded for my efforts.

My immense reward is described in this book. But what made Mahabharata researchers think that the duration of Bhishma on the bed of arrows was only 58 days? The answer can be found in this one reference of the Mahabharata text.

Anushasan (CE 153:27, GP 167:27)

अष्टपञ्चाशतं रात्र्यः शयानस्याद्य मे गताः |
शरेषु निशिताग्रेषु यथा वर्षशतं तथा ||२७||

When Yudhishthira arrived at Kurukshetra on the day of the

170

winter solstice, after spending 50 nights in Hastinapura, Bhishma told Yudhishthira that he felt the past 58 nights, while he was lying on the bed of arrows, as if equal to 100 years (a very long time).

That's it!

It is hard to conceive that merely based on one chronology reference, these researchers could have reached such a disastrous conclusion! Unfortunate indeed but true!

Is there any other way we can interpret this observation? We sure can. Recall what Krishna had said to Bhishma, the first time Yudhishthira and his party met Bhishma at Kurukshetra, after the coronation of Yudhishthira.

Shanti (CE 51:14, GP 51:14)

पञ्चाशतं षट्च कुरुप्रवीर; शेषं दिनानां तव जीवितस्य |
ततः शुभैः कर्मफलोदयैस्त्वं; समेष्यसे भीष्म विमुच्य देहम् ||१४||

Krishna told Bhishma that he had an additional 56 days to live, i.e, the day of the winter solstice was about 56 days away from the day of their conversation.

10.1.1 Truthlikeness Score of "-1"

Let's begin our analysis by stating the worst-case effect due to this evidence of 58 days for my claim. We may agree that per simplistic interpretation of the majority of Mahabharata researchers, this piece of evidence goes against my claim and thus Truthlikeness score for my proposal would go down by 1 point.

10.1.2 Reconciling 56 and 58 Days

This gap of 2 days between Krishna's assertion of 56 additional days for Bhishma to be on the bed of arrows and Bhishma's comment of his being on the bed of arrows for 58 days, can be reconciled in multiple ways.

10.1.2.1 Past/Latest 58 Days

A straightforward reading of this reference can be interpreted to mean that Bhishma is simply referring to the past 58 days of his time on the bed of arrows. Numerous Mahabharata researchers failed to grasp this fact simply because they never bothered to identify all relevant astronomy and chronology references related to Bhishma-nirvana. All of them are listed in Chapter 3 of this book.

10.1.2.2 Error in Prediction for the Day of Winter Solstice

An ordinary error in the prediction for the day of winter solstice and the actual day of the winter solstice can have an error of +/- one day. This is the same error we expect in the determination of the lunar tithi.

10.1.2.3 The Problem of Communication

In addition, it is not unsual to have an error of such magnitude (+/- 2) when the intent is communicated in colloquial terms (e.g., meeting after a week could be interpreted as either after seven or eight days).

An error of +/- two days can easily occur depending on the person's method of counting, i.e., whether he included both days - 1) the day of the discussion and 2) the actual day of Bhishma-nirvana or not.

10.1.2.4 Actual Scenario for the Year 5561 BCE

The Mahabharata war began on 16 October 5561 BCE and Bhishma fell in the battle on the 10th day of the war, i.e. on 25 October 5561 BCE. The war continued for an additional eight days until 2nd November 5561 BCE. Bhima and Arjuna humbled Ashwatthama on 3 November, and Yudhishthira and his party went to the bank of Ganga river on 4th November.

Yudhishthira and his party spent a month on the bank of Ganga river. Assuming they spent 29 days (duration of lunar month) at the Ganga river, they must have returned sometime on or after 2nd December. We will assume 2nd December, for the sake of our narration, as the day when they entered Hastinapura.

Yudhishthira was coronated as the King, and he assigned administrative posts to individuals and honored Krishna. Let's assume that the days of 2nd through 4th December were spent in these activities.

Yudhishthira and his brothers, along with Krishna and others, visited Bhishma at Kurukshetra on 5th December 5561 BCE. It is on this day that Krishna told Bhishma that the latter had 56 more days to live. In this case, we can interpret that Krishna was referring to the day of 30 January 5560 BCE, which was indeed 56 days away from this day.

On the other hand, when Bhishma referred to "past" 58 days, he referred to days from their first meeting (5 December) until the day (31 January 5560 BCE) when Bhishma spoke this statement, referring to his past 58 days on the bed of arrows.

10.1.3 Logic of Stepwise Regression – Value of an Evidence

Finally, I want to suggest a thought experiment to comprehend the value of each piece of evidence that leads to the total duration of Bhishma on the bed of arrows. The analogy I use is that of stepwise regression, where one data point can be selectively removed to see the effect of lack of that data point on the rest of the correlation.

Let's enumerate the quantifying evidence that goes into the calculation of the duration of Bhishma on the bed of arrows:

1. 9 days of the war when Bhishma was lying on the bed (10th through 18th day of the war)
2. Yudhishthira and his party on the bank of Ganga river for a month (27-30 days). We will use the most conservative estimate of 27 days.

3. Returning of Yudhishthira to Hastinapura, his coronation, and then his going to Bhishma at Kurukshetra. Let's designate this unknown interval = X days
4. Krishna tells Bhishma that Bhishma had 56 more days to live
5. Yudhishthira-Bhishma samvada begins and can be traced for at least 5 of the 6 days of its total duration
6. Yudhishthira went back to Hastinapura and stayed there for 50 nights before returning to Bhishma on the day of Bhishma-nirvana
7. Bhishma told Yudhishthira that he felt that the past 58 days on the bed of arrows as equal to 100 years (a long time).

Our thought experiment involves removing any one piece of evidence at a time and gauging the impact of its absence on our ability to draw the conclusion for the duration of Bhishma on the bed of arrows.

1. If we remove the reference to nine days of the war, we are still left with $27 + X + 56 = (83 + X)$ days
2. If we remove the reference to Yudhishthira on the bank of Ganga river for a month, we are still left with $9 + X + 56 = (65 + X)$ days
3. If we remove the reference to "X" days, we are left with $9 + 27 + 56 = 92$ days
4. If we remove the reference to Krishna stating Bhishma had 56 more days to live, we are still left with $9 + 27 + X + 5 + 50 = (91+X)$ days
5. If we remove the reference to narration of up to 5 days of Yudhishthira-Bhishma samvada, we are still left with $(92+X)$ days
6. If we remove the reference to Yudhishthira staying in Hastinpura for 50 nights, we are still left with $(92+X)$ days
7. If we remove the reference to Bhishma stating that he felt his duration of the past 58 days on the bed of arrows as being like a long time, we are still left with $(92+X)$ days.

8. If this one reference of 58 days is removed, we can still estimate the duration of Bhishma on the bed of arrows. In fact, removal of this one reference (not that I am suggesting it) will remove all the "apparent" confusion related to Bhishma-nirvana events. On the other hand, anyone insisting on 58 days has the onus to explain at least 59 specific references and the long narration that is carried over 8 long parvas (Bhishma through Anushasan) of the Mahabharata text. In addition, the context of Bhishma's statement of "58 days" can be easily explained. This is not possible for remaining references either individually or cumulatively that are spread over eight parvas.

What this thought experiment demonstrates is that the Mahabharata text evidence is very robust, and the removal of any one data point leads to the estimation of duration for Bhishma from being (65+X) days to (92+X) days. And this estimate is using the most conservative criterion. The actual duration was longer, since we don't know the exact value of "X"; however, we do know that it is not zero.

This thought experiment should make it clear to all and sundry that the decision to stick to one arbitrary (or selective) reference of Bhishma-nirvana was illogical, unscientific, and frankly, imprudent.

10.2 Bhishma-nirvana During Lunar Month of "Magha"

The majority of Mahabharata researchers insist that the lunar month at the time of Bhishma-nirvana was Magha. They base this claim based on one reference of the Mahabharata text.

Anushasan (CE 153:28, GP 167:28)

माघोऽयं समनुप्राप्तो मासः पुण्यो युधिष्ठिर।
त्रिभागशेषः पक्षोऽयं शुक्लो भवितुमर्हति ॥२८॥

175

Bhishma states that "it appears to be the auspicious month of Magha." Fortunately, the explanation for this discrepancy, at least for my claimed timing of 31 January 5560 BCE for the day of Bhishma-nirvana can be explained rather easily.

10.2.1 Truthlikeness Score of "-1"

Let's begin our analysis by stating the worst-case effect due to this evidence of "Magha" as the lunar month at the time of Bhishma-nirvana. We may agree that per simplistic interpretation of the majority of Mahabharata researchers, this piece of evidence goes against my claim, and thus, the Truthlikeness Score for my proposal would go down by one point.

10.2.2 Case of the Month to be something else than "Magha"

When we combine evidence that leads to 92+ days for the duration of Bhishma on the bed of arrows with evidence for the lower and upper tithis of Bhishma-nirvana, we realize that the lunar month of Bhishma-nirvana, , would be Phalguna, even Chaitra - at least in principle, but it can not be Magha. This is because the limits on the tithi of Bhishma-nirvana come out to be between Phalguna Shukla 12 and Chaitra Purnima.

10.2.3 Case of the Adhika Masa as an Explanation

If we assume Adhika masa occurring sometime during the year of the Mahabharata war, the month of Phalguna, purely based on the position of the full moon, could be designated as "Magha." Numerous Mahabharata researchers have made such an assumption.

My explanation for this mention of "Magha" when the month was "Phalguna" follows this logic. However, there is one additional explanation possible, and I prefer it over the assumption of 'Adhika masa,' again based on specific research which is beyond the purview of this book. However, I do want to mention the explanation.

176

10.2.4 Error due to Nomenclature of Lunar month(s)

It is not unusual to come across lunar month names in our modern Hindu calendars where occasionally, the name of the lunar month, when compared against the position of the corresponding full moon, appears inappropriate. For example, I have noted instances when the full moon is very near nakshatra Magha; however, the month is still named as 'Pausha'.

Granted, this could be more likely the effect of the Adhika-masa correction happening in that year. But then, do recall that the Adhika masa correction is occurring on an average every 2.5 years, and thus such instances of mismatch between the naming of a lunar month and the corresponding position of a full moon are common.

10.3 Bhishma-nirvana on Magha Shukla Ashtami (8)

Anushasan (CE 153:28, GP 167:28)

माघोऽयं समनुप्राप्तो मासः पुण्यो युधिष्ठिर |
त्रिभागशेषः पक्षोऽयं शुक्लो भवितुमर्हति ||२८||

I deliberately separated the issues related to this reference of the Mahabharata text into two parts: 1) lunar month of Magha (10.3) and 2) Magha Shukla Ashtami (10.3).

After stating that "the month appears to be Magha," Bhishma continued and stated (second line of the shloka) that:

> "the timing appeared to be when 3 parts (or 1/3 part) of the paksha (fortnight or month) were remaining (or has elapsed)."

Mahabharata researchers have written much in interpreting this one line. In fact, there are too many interpretations with every conceivable permutation and combination one can imagine. We will summarize them:

10.3.1 Lunar Month of Magha or Phalguna

We will resolve the issue of nomenclature or designation of the lunar month as described in section 10.2. If the month of Bhishma-nirvana is +/- one month from Magha, we will accept it as corroborated. The actual difference could be due to insertion of Adhika masa or simply due to an error in nomenclature/designation.

We will focus solely on paksha and tithi in the remainder of this discussion.

10.3.2 Paksha or Masa? 1/3 or 1/4? Elapsed or Remaining?

त्रिभागशेष: has been interpreted in multiple ways – 1/3 or 1/4, and again 2/3 and 3/4! The confusion does not stop here. There is no agreement among researchers as to whether this fraction applies to the Paksha (lunar fortnight) or to the month. Depending on the interpretation selected, we have a series of dates that can be briefly summarized as (1) Shukla 3, (2) Shukla 4, (3) Shukla 5, (4) Shukla 8 (5) Shukla 12 and again, these tithis repeated for Krishna/Vadya paksha, i.e., Krishna 3, 4, 5, 8, and 12.

Adding to this commotion, a reasonable error in the determination of tithis for a time much farther into antiquity (considering the unpredictable movement of the moon coupled with changes in the rotation of the earth contributing to unknown "Delta T" correction desired), we can practically imagine tithis (of both paksha) from dwitiya (2) through navami (9) and ekadashi (11) through trayodashi (13).

In effect, any tithi will do if it is not pratipada (1), Amavasya (15), dashami (10), chaturdashi (14) or Purnima (15)! Having said that, the assumption of Magha Shukla Ashtami (8) has attained a certain status, and therefore we will deal with it separately.

10.3.3 Magha Shukla Ashtami (8)

One of the interpretations from 10.3.2 naturally leads to Magha Shukla 8. However, it appears that the interpretation by Nilkantha

Chaturdhar, the Mahabharata commentator of 17th century CE, is responsible for its popularity.

In commenting on this reference, Nilkantha Chaturdhar wrote:

माघोऽयमिति सौम्यश्चान्द्रः मासस्य चतुर्भागकरणे साधसप्तभागत्वात् अष्टम्यर्धस्यानतीतत्वेन प्रथमभागस्य विद्यमानत्वात् त्रिभागशेषो भवितुमर्हतीत्यर्थः तेनाद्याष्टमीत्यर्थः ।

In brief, if you divide the lunar month (30 days) in 4 parts, each part would amount to 7.5 days and per his (Chaturdhar) interpretation, 1/4 portion had elapsed and 3/4 were remaining. This would mean it was the tithi of Magha Shukla 8.

To make reader aware of the complexity involved in the interpretation of this shloka, I will quote a comment of Shri Nityanada Mishra from one of the discussions (very much related to this verse of the Mahabharata text) on one of the online forums – "भारतीयविद्वत्परिषत्." Shri Nityananda Mishra writes:

Is that the complete commentary or is something missing? We do not see any अन्वय nor do we see the explanation of पक्षः शुक्लः so it is not certain what is the अन्वय taken by नीलकण्ठ. I do not have the source to check with me.

Any interpretation, especially a claim like this means पूर्णिमान्त or अमावस्यान्त, must be backed by complete parsing and grammatical analysis of the verse. Without an अन्वय and without an explanation of each and every term, we are just building castles in the air.

As we see two अयं terms, there seem to be two वाक्यs. The अन्वय then becomes very important. Is त्रिभागशेषः to be taken with the first sentence as the adjective of मासः or as the adjective of पक्षः in the second sentence? A possible अन्वय (there may be other possibilities too) is (हे) युधिष्ठिर. अयं सौम्यः माघः मासः समनुप्राप्तः (अस्ति). अयं त्रिभागशेषः पक्षः शुक्लः भवितुमर्हति. As per my limited knowledge there should be two nouns (not counting adjectives) in

179

nominative singular in the second sentence - so that we have [X] [Y] भवितुम् अर्हति. If त्रिभागशेषः is to be taken with the मासः in previous sentence, then what are the two nouns in the second sentence? And if भवितुम् अर्हति is taken with मासः (as seems from the possibly incomplete quotation of the commentary) and the whole verse is taken as one वाक्य, then why are two अयं terms used? Another important point is how is भवितुम् अर्हति to be interpreted and as per what Paninian rules. Specifically, what is the कर्ता for भवितुम् अर्हति and in what sense भवितुम् अर्हति is used, is it used in the sense of भवति or भविष्यति or some other sense.

This selective reference and its arbitrary interpretation led almost all Mahabharata researchers onto the wrong track. We will discuss the consequence of this unfortunate event in the next chapter.

10.3.4 Magha Shukla 4 or Magha Krishna 4

Bharat-ratna and Mahamahopadhya - P.V. Kane interpreted it as Magha Shukla 8 and suggested two additional possibilities. In his words:

> The difficulty is how to connect 'त्रिभागशेषः,' whether as an adjective of 'masa' or of 'paksha'. If we take it in the first way, these words were uttered on 8th of Magha Shukla. If we take it as n adjective of 'paksha', then they will have to be taken as uttered on the 4th of the bright half or on the 4th of the dark half which may be regarded in its astrological effects as equal to 'shuklapaksha' (though the tithi itself is in the dark half).

In effect, he considered Magha Shukla 4, Magha Shukla 8, and Magha Krishna 4 as three possible interpretations. Do recognize that with the assumption of correction to the name of the month either due to adhika masa or simply due to nomenclature error, this can turn this into Phalugna Shukla 4, 8 or Phalguna Krishna 4.

I may mention that 31 January 5560 BCE, my proposed day of

180

Bhishma-nirvana, indeed was the day of Phalguna Krishna 4. It was also the day after the day of the winter solstice - 30 January 5560 BCE.

10.4 Timing of Krishna's Peace Mission Before the War

We have shown how the timing of the Mahabharta war itself was during the first half of Sharad season. There is one reference in the Mahabharata text that conflicts with this conclusion.

Udyoga (CE 81:6-7, GP 83:6-7)

ततो व्यपेते तमसि सूर्ये विमल उद्गते ।
मैत्रे मुहूर्ते सम्प्राप्ते मृद्वर्चिषि दिवाकरे ॥६॥

कौमुदे मासि रेवत्यां शरदन्ते हिमागमे ।
स्फीतसस्यमुखे काले कल्यः सत्त्ववतां वरः ॥७॥

Long before the war, Krishna left from Upaplavya and went to Hastinpura on a peace mission to explore whether the war could be avoided. The Mahabharata text states the timing of this instance as that of "at the end of Sharad season and at the beginning of Hemanta season." This reference certainly conflicts with our assertions that the timing of the war was that of the early Sharad season. The event of Krishna leaving from Upaplavya was long before the war.

The entire chronology evidence of Bhishma on the bed of arrows for more than 92 days goes against the claim of this one reference. The entire evidence of Sharad season descriptions throughout the 18 days of the war also goes against this claim of one reference.

The Mahabharata text also allows us to estimate the chronological timing of Krishna's leaving from Upaplavya at least 15 days and as much as 45 days before the first day of the war. The requirement of at least 42 days comes from another reference of

181

Balarama's Tirthayatra, where he left for the Sarasvati river, only after Krishna's return back to Upaplavya after a failed peace mission. Balarama left the Pandava camp on nakshatra Anuradha and then traveled along the Sarasvati river for 42 days before returning to Kurukshetra on the last and 18th day of the war to witness the club fight between Bhima and Duryodhana. This means that when we include Balarama's Tirthayatra in our chronology consideration, Krishna's leaving from Upaplavyas was at least (42 + 18 + 30+X + 56) days, i.e., (136 + X) days before the day of Bhishma-nirvana and that would mean at least 15 days into Varsha season!

Without going into the solution(s) of "Balarama's Tirthayatra" problem, it is enough to emphasize that there is enormous evidence against this lone reference which demands Krishna leaving from Upaplavya on a peace mission at the end of Sharad season.

Those who are curious about the problem of "Balarama Tirthayatra", may read my first book.

10.5 Shakra Amavasya and First Day of Mahabharata War

Krishna tells Karna that Shakra Amavasya would occur in seven days, and either the "war preparations" or the "war itself" could begin on this day.

Udyoga (CE 140:18, GP 142:18)

सप्तमाच्चापि दिवसादमावास्या भविष्यति |
सङ्ग्रामं योजयेत्रत तां ह्याहुः शक्रदेवताम् ॥१८॥

The problem of "Shakra Amavasya" is rather peripheral to the subject of Bhishma-nirvana and is discussed here for the sake of completeness. Whether the war began in seven days from the time of Krishna-Karna samvada, or after a month and seven days, does have implications for corroborating "Tirthayatra of Balarama"; however, it does not have direct implication for the chronology of Bhishma-nirvana.

10.6 Late Moonrise on the 14th Day of the War

We have shown that the observations of the Mahabharata text, when analyzed judiciously, lead to the stringent condition of Kartika Amavasya as the first day of the Mahabharata war. This means the majority of the war took place during the Shukla paksha of Margashirsha. Thus, the 14th day of the war would be near Purnima, and thus the claim that the moon rose late into the night conflicts with the evidence for the phases and positions of the moon through the 18 days of the war.

I would encourage curious readers to read my first book for the explanation of this "apparent" late moonrise. The only reason I included this observation into the list of conflicting observations is because it conflicts with the assertion of Kartika Amavasya as the first day of the war, Shukla paksha of Margashirsha when the majority of the war took place, and that the 14th day of the war must be near full moon day, and thus, nowhere close to the day that would result in a late moonrise.

Summary

Bhishma's reference to 58 days can be easily understood in the context of his referring to the past 58 days leading to the day of Bhishma-nirvana and not to the total duration of him on the bed of arrows. On the other hand, anyone assuming 58 days to be the total duration of Bhishma on the bed of arrows would land in all kinds of illogical inferences. We will indeed see a demonstration of this in the next chapter.

The problem of nomenclature of the month (Magha or Phalguna) is rather easy to solve. Correction of adhika masa can lead to such an error. The error of +/- one month, in the nomenclature of lunar month, occurs frequently even in our times and can be validated by referring to the modern Hindu panchanga (calendar).

The problem of tithi and its solution leads to multiple choices, and my claimed date of 31 January 5560 BCE for the day of Bhishma-nirvana agrees with one of the many choices, including the interpretation by late P. V. Kane.

183

11

Superficial and Manipulative Claims

"The test of originality for an idea is not the absence of one single predecessor but the presence of multiple but incompatible ones."
- Nassim Nicholas Taleb

Let's revisit the Grains & Chaff Separation Matrix™ to refresh ourselves on the definition of "superficial & manipulative claims."

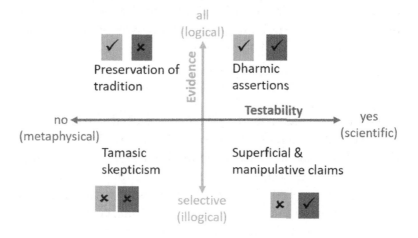

A claim that empirically tests arbitrary or selective set of data but avoids testing and analyzing all relevant evidence is termed as a 'superficial and manipulative' claim.

The "superficial" aspect of these claims is the illogical and unscientific decision, deliberate or ignorant, to include and test only arbitrary or selective sets of evidence while avoiding, deliberately or ignorantly, the inclusion, analysis, and testing of all relevant data.

A researcher who produces such claims is termed as, without

assigning any motive to his actions, a 'superficial manipulator.'

Most claims for the year of the Mahabharata war (125+) fall into this 4th quadrant of 'superficial and manipulative' claims.

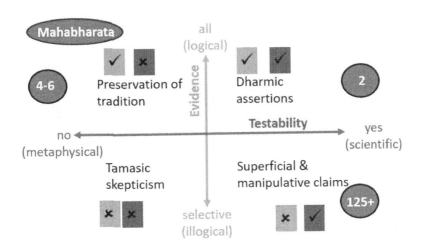

For brevity, we will analyze only those claims that have proposed the first day of the Mahabharata war and the day of Bhishma-nirvana.

Mahabharata Researcher	10th day of the War (claim) (*Gregorian)	Day of Bhishma Nirvana (claim)	Day of Winter solstice (*Gregorian)
V M Shaligram	27 October 5774 BCE*	24 December 5774 BCE*	17 December 5774 BCE*
P V Vartak	25 October 5561 BCE	22 December 5561 BCE	30 January 5560 BCE
Vedveer Arya	3 November 3163 BCE	31 December 3163 BCE	14 January 3162 BCE
P V Holay	22 November 3143 BCE	18 January 3142 BCE	14 January 3142 BCE
Saroj Bala	22 October 3140 BCE*	19 December 3140 BCE*	19 December 3140 BCE*
K S Raghavan Narahari Achar	1 December 3067 BCE	17 January 3066 BCE	13 January 3066 BCE
P C Sengupta	13 November 2449 BCE	15 Jan 2448 BCE	8 January 2448 BCE
Anand Sharan	9 November 2156 BCE	6 January 2155 BCE	7 January 2155 BCE
Mohan Gupta	26 October 1952 BCE	23 December 1952 BCE	5 January 1951 BCE
Ashok Bhatnagar	23 October 1793 BCE*	20 December 1793 BCE*	20 December 1793 BCE*

These claims rely on selective evidence of "58 days" and/or the lunar tithi of Bhishma-nirvana to be that of Magha Shukla 8. Implicit in these two assumptions (of Nilkantha Chaturdhar) is also the implicit assumption of the war beginning on the day of Kartika Amavasya.

We will award one point each for satisfying the condition of 58 days (+/- one day) and the condition of Magha Shukla 8 (+/- one day), provided the day of Bhishma-nirvana so claimed (even though based on an illogical premise of two selective references) falls on the day of the winter solstice (+/- one day). This is because corroborating the requirement of the winter solstice is crucial for any claim of Bhishma-nirvana.

Anushasan (CE 153:27-28, GP 167:27-28)

अष्टपञ्चाशतं रात्र्यः शयानस्याद्य मे गताः |
शरेषु निशिताग्रेषु यथा वर्षशतं तथा ||२७||

माघोऽयं समनुप्राप्तो मासः पुण्यो युधिष्ठिर |
त्रिभागशेषः पक्षोऽयं शुक्लो भवितुमर्हति ||२८||

Most of the researchers, although not all, who made these claims are still around. I kindly encourage and request them to critique my work. They must provide rebuttal to my criticism of their specific claims and provide the explanation of why they chose only selective evidence. It will be interesting to see, if they remain convinced of their claims, even after analyzing my work and my criticism of their research. My prediction is that most of them, if not all, will avoid responding. This is because to reject my date would amount to rejecting Mahabharata evidence.

We will analyze the claims beginning with the oldest date (year) proposed.

11.1 V.M. Shaligram

Bhishma-nirvana claim
24 December 5774 BCE - <u>Gregorian</u> reference calendar

Shaligram proposed 18 October 5774 BCE as the first day of the Mahabharata war. This means the 10th day of the war when Bhishma fell in the battle was 27 October 5774 BCE. Shaligram claimed 24 December 5774 BCE as the day of Bhishma-nirvana. The day happens to be Chaitra Shukla Ekadashi.

The motivation to select 24 December appears to be driven by his desire to corroborate the selective reference of 58 days, i.e., from 27 October through 24 December. On the the other hand, the actual day of the winter solstice was seven to six days earlier (17 December 5774 BCE), and thus, Shaligram keeps Bhishma waiting on the bed of arrows, unnecessarily, for an additional five to six days.

The lunar tithis for the timeline of Shaligram are completely out of whack. His first day of the war is on Magha Shukla 4 and Bhishma-nirvana on Chaitra Shukla 11!

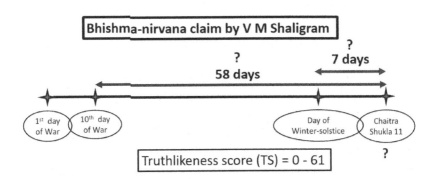

187

11.2 5561 BCE

We will discuss the claim of Dr. P.V. Vartak and my claim in this section, since both of us agree on the year 5561 BCE for the year of Mahabharata war and since both of us also agree on the 18-day long timeline of the Mahabharata war beginning with 16 October 5561 BCE through 2 November 55601 BCE. On the other hand, the day of Bhisha-nirvana claimed by us are separated by 40 days.

11.2.1 P.V. Vartak

Bhishma-nirvana claim
22 December 5561 BCE – Confused reference calendar

Vartak proposed 16 October 5561 BCE (per Julian calendar reference) as the first day of the Mahabharta war. This means the 10th day of the war was 25 October 5561 BCE. Vartak claimed 22 December 5561 BCE (per confused calendar reference) as the day of Bhishma-nirvana. The day happens to be Magha Shukla 8.

The motivation to select 22 December appears to be driven by his desire to corroborate the selective reference of 58 days, i.e., from 25 October through 22 December and the tithi of Magha Shukla 8. Vartak was indeed aware of numerous additional Bhishma-nirvana references from the Mahabharata text. Unfortunately, he misinterpreted them forcefully to fit the duration of 58 days and failed miserably.

On the other hand, the actual day of winter solstice was 40 days away, in the future (30/31 January 5560 BCE). Vartak also confused himself and his readers by following the Julian calendar for the rest of his work, while jumping suddenly and illogically to the Gregorian calendar to state the day of Bhishma-nirvana. It is worth mentioning that the day of the winter solstice in the year 5561 BCE, per Gregorian calendar, occurred on 17 December and not on 22 December. A massive disaster on all fronts!

188

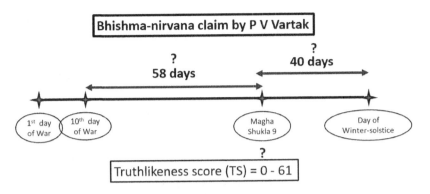

11.2.2 Nilesh N. Oak

Bhishma-nirvana claim
31 January 5560 BCE – <u>Julian</u> reference calendar

Since I have accepted Vartak's timeline for the 18 days of the war (16 October -2 November 5561 BCE), I will discuss my date of 31 December 5560 BCE for the day of Bhishma-nirvana.

My claim of 31 January 5560 BCE corroborates all the evidence of Bhishma-nirvana, especially when we consider explanations and multiple interpretations discussed in Chapter 10.

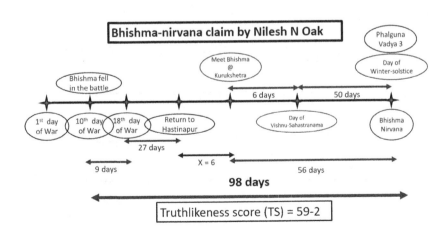

However, since two references of 58 days and Magha Shukla 8 have been so convincingly <u>misinterpreted</u> for more than 300 years (beginning with Nilkantha Chaturdhar in the late 17th century all the way to our times), I count 2 points against my claim, as a friendly concession to laziness of other Mahabharata researchers.

My Truthlikeness Score (TS) = 59-2

11.3 Vedveer Arya

Bhishma-nirvana claim
31 December 3163 BCE - <u>Julian</u> reference calendar

Vedveer Arya proposed 25 October 3163 BCE as the first day of the Mahabharata war. This means the 10th day of the war when Bhishma fell in the battle was 3 November 3163 BCE. Vedveer Arya claimed 31 December 3163 BCE as the day of Bhishma-nirvana. The day happens to be Magha Shukla 8.

The motivation to select 31 December appears to be driven by his desire to corroborate the selective references of 58 days, i.e., from 3 November through 31 December and the tithi of Magha Shukla 8.

On the the other hand, the actual day of winter solstice was 14 days into the future (14 January 3162 BCE), and thus, Vedveer Arya forces Bhishma to leave his body at least 14 days earlier than Bhishma's desired day of the winter solstice!

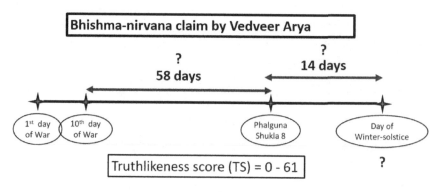

190

11.4 P.V. Holay

Bhishma-nirvana claim
18 January 3142 BCE – <u>Julian</u> reference calendar

Holay proposed 13 November 3143 BCE as the first day of the Mahabharata war. This means the 10th day of the war when Bhishma fell in the battle was 22 November 3143 BCE. Holay claimed 18 January 3142 BCE as the day of Bhishma-nirvana.

The motivation to select 18 January appears to be driven by his desire to corroborate the selective references of 58 days and Magha Shukla 8. The tithi for 18 January was Phalguna Shukla 7.

The actual day of the winter solstice was four days earlier (14 January) than the day claimed by Holay for the day of Bhishma-nirvana.

In addition, Holay was forced to make a baseless (i.e., no evidence) conjecture of the war stopping after Bhishma's fall in the battle for 12 days(!) before it resumed. The Mahabharata text has enormous evidence to show that the war took place consecutively for 18 days. This is a good illustration of desperate levels attempted by Mahabharata researchers to corroborate two selective references of 58 days and Magaha Shukla 8.

I suggest that there should be an additional category of assigning negative points for suggesting a conjecture that has no basis, but rather contradicts enormous existing evidence.

However, let's recognize an ingenious, although erroneous, attempt of Late Shri Holay, an astronomer par excellence. By introducing, albeit unjustifiable, gap of 12 days after the fall of Bhishma, he tried to match 58 days and Magha Shukla 8 for his claimed day for Bhishma-nirvana. This imaginary conjecture was also his attempt to explain the "alleged" late moonrise observation on the 14th day of the war and to match irreconcilable observations of 'Tirthayatra of Balarama'.

Holay is not alone in making such baseless conjectures. We may have an opportunity to identify a few additional ones by other researchers before this chapter is over.

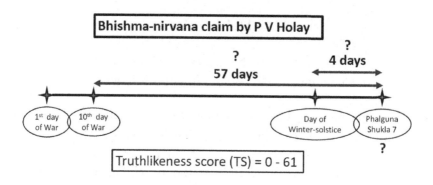

11.5 Saroj Bala

Bhishma-nirvana claim
19 December 3140 BCE – <u>Gregorian</u> reference calendar

Saroj Bala proposed 13 October 3140 BCE as the first day of the Mahabharata war. This means the 10th day of the war when Bhishma fell in the battle was 22 October 3140 BCE. Bala claimed 19 December 3140 BCE as the day of Bhishma-nirvana. That day happens to be Phalguna Shukla 6.

The motivation to select 19 December appears to be driven by her desire to corroborate the selective reference of 58 days, i.e., from 22 October through 19 December.

The Mahabharata text states in no uncertain terms that Duryodhana was killed on the 18th day of the war. On the other hand, Bala was forced to make a baseless assumption of Duryodhana running away from the battle on the 18th day of war and was being found out 12 days later (i.e, 12 days after the last or 18th day of the war). I am confident readers will have their own déjà vu moment! While Late Shri Holay stopped the war for 12 days after the 10th day of the war, Bala extended the war by 12 days after the 18th and last day of the war! Both attempts are in-genious, yet ultimately unsuccessful efforts to corroborate irreconcilable observations of 'Tirthayatra of Balarama'.

It is important to realize the common thread among these re-searchers – the common factor of having a priori conclusion/claim for the year of Mahabharata war which then is justified by twisting

192

and torturing the evidence including insertion of imaginary events not mentioned in the Mahabharata text.

Since this false conjecture of extending the war by 12 days have no direct effect on Bhishma-nirvana and the fact that the day of Bhishma-nirvana claimed by Bala does occur on the day of the winter solstice, we can count 1 point in favor of her proposal in our calculations of Truthlikeness score.

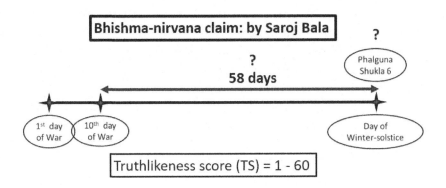

11.6 Srinivas Raghavan

Bhishma Nirvana claim
17 January 3066 BCE – <u>Julian</u> reference calendar

11.6.1 Srinivas Raghavan

K Srinivasa Raghavan proposed 22 November 3067 BCE as the first day of the Mahabharata war. This means the 10th day of the war when Bhishma fell in the battle was 1 December 3067 BCE. Raghavan claimed 17 January 3066 BCE as the day of Bhishma-nirvana. The day happens to be Phalguna Shukla 7.

It is impossible to determine what were the motivations of Raghavan in proposing any of these dates! He proposed the first day of the war that occurs on Shukla Ekadashi (+/- one tithi), probably based on a traditional yet erroneous date of Gita-jayanti

(Margashirsha Shukla Ekadashi). The evidence of the Mahabharata text is decisive on Kartika Amavasaya as the first day of the war. It is not a surprise that the entire endeavor of Prof. Raghavan to determine the year of the Mahabharta war is a downhill journey with no chance for recovery! We will limit ourselves to discussing only those blunders that relate to the events of Bhishma-nirvana.

Raghavan focused only on selective evidence of 58 days and Magha Shukla 8; however, he ran into additional difficulties because of his false start for the day of the Mahabharata war, which in turn was based on 'traditional belief' rather than internal evidence of the Mahabharata text.

He tried to save his claim from this predicament by translating the reference of 58 days in an innovative fashion. It is not clear if Prof. Raghavan requested this individual - Sriman Vidwan Melma Narasimha Thathacharya swamigal avl. - or if Sriman Swamigal had translated this reference earlier, and Prof. Raghavan simply came across it.

Sriman Vidwan Melma Narasimha Thathacharya swawmigal avl. translated reference of 58 days as:

> Bhishma, who was on the bed of arrows, said, "I have not slept for 58 days" from the day he was made the General of the Kaurva army!

Unfortunately, even such extreme juggling and torturing of evidence was not sufficient. The Mahabharata text has clear references that show that the day when Bhishma was made the General of the Kaurava army, was long before the first day of the war, and not just the day before the war. For example, Bhishma was made a General of the Kaurava army long before the first day of Mahabharata war.

Udyoga (CE 148:1-4, GP 150:1-4)

वासुदेव उवाच||
एवमुक्ते तु भीष्मेण द्रोणेन विदुरेण च |
गान्धार्या धृतराष्ट्रेण न च मन्दोऽन्वबुध्यत ||१||

194

अवधूयोत्थितः क्रुद्धो रोषात्संरक्तलोचनः |
अन्वद्रवन्त तं पश्चाद्राजानस्त्यक्तजीविताः ||२||

अज्ञापयच्च राजस्तान्पार्थिवान्दुष्टचेतसः |
प्रयाध्वं वै कुरुक्षेत्रं पुष्योऽद्येति पुनः पुनः ||३||

ततस्ते पृथिवीपालाः प्रययुः सहसैनिकाः |
भीष्मं सेनापतिं कृत्वा संहृष्टाः कालचोदिताः ||४||

And

Udyoga (CE 153:26, GP 156:26)

वैशम्पायन उवाच||
ततः सेनापतिं चक्रे विधिवद्भूरिदक्षिणम् |
धृतराष्ट्रात्मजो भीष्मं सोऽभिषिक्तो व्यरोचत ||२६||

And then the Kauravas went to Kurukshetra and established
their base at Kurukshetra.

Udyoga (CE 153:34-35, GP 156: 34-35)

परिक्रम्य कुरुक्षेत्रं कर्णेन सह कौरवः |
शिबिरं मापयामास समे देशे नराधिपः ||३४||

मधुरानूषरे देशे प्रभूतयवसेन्धने |
यथैव हास्तिनपुरं तद्वच्छिबिरमाबभौ ||३५||

After this incident, the Pandavas chose their general, and then

195

headed for Kurukshetra and established their base. There are various other instances of Balarama who visited Kurukshetra and left for 'Tirthayatra'on Maitri (Anuradha) nakshatra followed by the visit of Rukmi and his departure, and this is when Duryodhana sent Uluka to the Pandava camp. The bottom line is, there was a significant interval between the day when Bhishma was made the General of the Kaurava army and the first day of the war.

This incorrect translation could not save Prof. Raghavan's claim. Per this new interpretation, he assumed that Bhishma had not slept from the first day of the Mahabharata war! Even with this incorrect interpretation, Prof. Raghavan could not show how there were 58 days from the first day of Mahabharata war to the day of the winter solstice. Even assuming Bhishma did not sleep from the night before the first day of the war until the day of winter solstice, i.e., from 21 November through 13 January (day of the winter solstice), it still amounts to only 54 days and not 58 days!

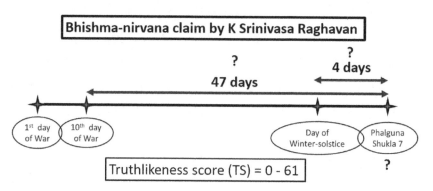

Raghavan had to force Bhishma to stay on the bed of arrows for more than four days beyond the day of the winter solstice to corroborate the condition of 58 days and Magha Shukla 8! Raghavan published his work in 1969 CE.

11.6.2 Narahari Achar

About 30 years after the work of Prof. Raghavan, Prof. Achar came on the scene, and despite all the problems described here, declared that he (Achar) had tested the claims of Prof. Raghavan. Not only did Prof. Achar fail to comprehend serious issues related to the claim of Prof. Raghavan, but dogmatically declared 3067 BCE as the year of the Mahabharata war.

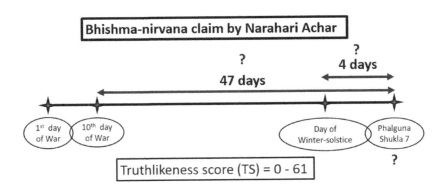

11.6.3 Manish Pandit

Unfortunately, the story of 3067 BCE is not over yet. Shri Manish Pandit, a medical professional and a good filmmaker, claims that he has verified the claims of Prof. Achar and he is convinced that 3067 BCE is the year of the Mahabharata war and is busy making a documentary film on this very date!

Let's be ready, with this book in hand, to enjoy the film of Shri Manish Pandit, when (and if) it is released.

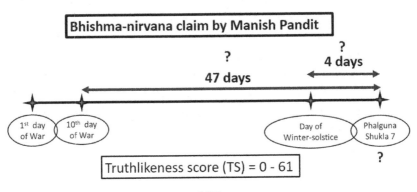

11.7 P. C. Sengupta

Bhishma-nirvana claim
15 January 2448 BCE – <u>Julian</u> reference calendar

Sengutpa proposed 4 Novemer 2449 BCE as the first day of the Mahabharata war. This means the 10th day of the war when Bhishma fell in the battle was 13 Novemer 2449 BCE. Sengupta claimed 15 January 2448 BCE as the day of Bhishma-nirvana. The day happens to be Magha Krishna 12.

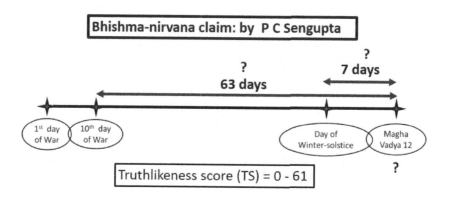

Sengupta shows, like Dr. Vartak, awareness of additional observations related to Bhishma-nirvana. He twists, turns, and misinterprets the chronology narratives and arrives after much confusion, claiming15 January 2448 BCE as the day of Bhishma-nirvana. His motivation for claiming 15 January is due to his colossal confusion with the reference of Krishna stating Bhishma had 56 additional days to live.

On the the other hand, the actual day of the winter solstice was six-seven days before (8 January 2448 BCE) and thus, Sengupta keeps Bhishma waiting on the bed of arrows unnecessarily for six-seven additional days.

198

11.8 Anand Sharan

Bhishma-nirvana claim
6 January 2155 BCE – <u>Julian</u> reference calendar

Anand Sharan proposed 31 October 2156 BCE as the first day of the Mahabharata war. This means the 10th day of the war when Bhishma fell in the battle was 9 November BCE. Prof. Sharan claimed 6 January 2155 BCE as the day of Bhishma-nirvana. The day happens to be Magha Krishna 2.

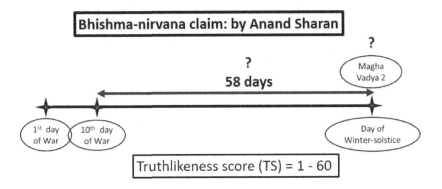

There are about 58 days, per the claim of Prof. Sharan for the duration of Bhishma on the bed of arrows. Thus, he could corroborate 1 selective reference out of 61+ references of Bhishma-nirvana.

11.9 Mohan Gupta

Bhishma-nirvana claim
23 December 1952 BCE – <u>Julian</u> reference calendar

Mohan Gupta proposed 17 October 1952 BCE as the first day of the Mahabharata war. This means the 10th day of the war when Bhishma fell in the battle was 26 October 1952 BCE. Prof. Gupta claimed 23 December 1952 BCE as the day of Bhishma-nirvana. The day happens to be Magha Shukla 8.

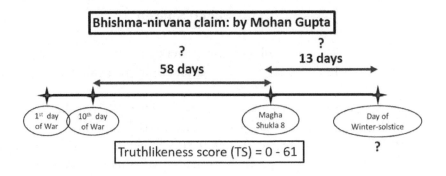

The motivation to select 23 December appears to be driven by his desire to corroborate the selective reference of 58 days, i.e., from 26 October through 23 December and to match the second selective reference of Magha Shukla 8. On the the other hand, the actual day of the winter solstice was 13 days into the future (5 January 1951 BCE), and thus, Prof. Gupta forces Bhishma to leave his body at least 13 days earlier than Bhishma's desired day of the winter solstice!

11.10 Ashok Bhatnagar

Bhishma-nirvana claim
20 December 1793 BCE – <u>Gregorian</u> reference calendar

Ashok Bhatnagar proposed 14 October 1793 BCE as the first day of the Mahabharata war. This means the 10th day of the war when Bhishma fell in the battle was 23 October 1793 BCE. Shri Bhatnagar claimed 20 December 1793 BCE as the day of Bhishma-nirvana. The day happens to be Magha Shukla 9.

The motivation to select 24 December appears to be driven by his desire to corroborate the selective reference of 58 days, i.e., from 23 October through 20 December and the selective reference of Magha Shukla 8. He shows ignorance of 59 additional chronology observations of Bhishma-nirvana. The day of 20 December 1793 BCE is within +/- one day of the day of the winter solstice. Thus, Bhatnagar's claim scores 2 points.

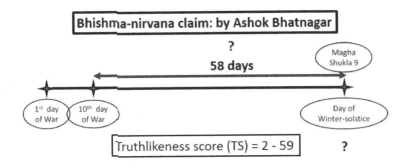

Summary

Most Mahabharata researchers (120+) do not bother to determine the day of Bhishma-nirvana. They are clueless of the importance of Bhishma-nirvana in determining the year of the Mahabharata war.

Few (10+) researchers who do show inclination to determine the day of Bhishma-nirvana exhibit obsessive-compulsive focus on two selective references out of ~61 specific references related to Bhishma-nirvana and thus, exhibit compulsive and illogical disregard towards 59+ relevant references of Bhishma-nirvana. Naturally, their claims for Bhishma-nirvana cannot corroborate most of references of the Mahabharata text. To make it worse, many of them are not aware of additional references related to Bhishma-nirvana, and even after becoming aware of them, they have failed to realize the falsification of their claims.

Two researchers, Dr. Vartak and Prof. Sengupta, showed awareness of some of the additional references (in addition to two selective references of 58 days and Magha Shukla 8) of Bhishma-nirvana. While Dr. Vartak interpreted them to suit the claim of 58 days, Prof. Sengupta twisted and interpreted one specific reference of 56 days to reach a misleading conclusion.

All researchers discussed in this chapter, showed obsessive compulsive focus for 2 of the 61+ observations - (1) '58' days duration and (2) Magha Shukla 8 for the day of Bhishma-nirvana.

The evidence of this book decisively falsifies all existing claims for the day and year of Bhishma-nirvana! Yes, you read that right!

12

Implications and Growth of Knowledge

"Science is not about control. It is about cultivating a perpetual condition of wonder in the face of something that forever grows one step richer and subtler than our latest theory about it. It is about reverence, not mastery."
- Richard Powers

Superior theory and/or superior claim explains more and is better tested. Every worthwhile new theory/claim leads to new predictions which in turn may lead to new problems. Frankly, the worth of a new theory can be measured by new problems, i.e., problems of an ever-increasing depth and an ever-increasing fertility. The lasting contribution to the growth of scientific knowledge that a new theory and claim can make is the new problems it raises.

12.1 Three Astronomy Poison Pills

Arundhati-Vasishtha (AV) observation is the first astronomy poison pill. The evidence of Bhishma-nirvana has produced two additional astronomy poison pills. These three poison pills destroy the myth that my claim for the year 5561 BCE, as the year of the Mahabharata war, was solely based on only one key Mahabharata observation of Arundhati-Vasishtha (AV).

12.1.1 Arundhati-Vasishtha (AV) Observation

The scientific testing of the Arundhati-Vasishtha (AV) observation had produced an interval of about 6500 years (11091 BCE – 4508 BCE) for the epoch of the Mabharata war.

12.1.2 Bhishma-nirvana

The evidence of lower and upper limits for Bhishma-nirvana produced an interval of about 4300 years (8000 BCE – 3700 BCE) for the epoch of Bhishma-nirvana, and thus, the Mahabharata war. The combining of these two inferences would produce an overlapping interval of about 3500 years (8000 BCE – 4508 BCE).

12.1.3 Margashirsha and First Half of Sharad Season

The evidence of war occurring during the lunar month of Margashirsha and during the first half of Sharad season produced an interval of about 2000 years (6722 BCE - 4562 BCE).

The evidence of war taking place during the Shukla paskha of Margashirsha and during the first half of Sharad season produced a refined interval of about 2000 years (7285 BCE - 5125 BCE).

These multiple intervals, together, tighten the interval to about 1600 years (5125 BCE – 6722 BCE) for the epoch of Bhishma-nirvana, and thus, the Mahabharata war.

The year of the Mahabharata war (5561 BCE) indeed falls within this crisp and narrow interval of 1600 years.

12.2 Alternate Claims of Mahabharata Chronology are False

These three astronomy poison pills falsify all alternate claims (130+) for the year of the Mahabharata war. Either of these poison pills, individually, or in various combinations, achieve this mighty feat! This is indeed the power of astronomy poison pills!

12.3 AIT or AMT is False

Aryan invasion theory (AIT) or Aryan migration theory (AMT) is not a theory, but a dogma. The proponents of this dogma try hanging on to any last straw to keep it active. The havoc created by AIT, as a destructive force for the unity of India, is well known and will not be discussed. The dogma of AIT/AMT has four specific claims:

1. There were people who called themselves "Aryan" and lived outside India
2. These "Aryans" migrated from somewhere outside India into greater India
3. This happened some time after 2000 BCE and before 1000 BCE
4. These "Aryans" brought the Sanskrit language or the precursor to Sanskrit languages, with them, to India

If we can demonstrate that a Sanskrit-based culture existed and flourished in India long before 2000 BCE, then the dogma of AIT/AMT is destroyed.

The astronomy poison pills discovered in this book convincingly show the existence of a flourishing Sanskrit-based culture in the sixth millennium BCE, and thus, destroy the dogma of AIT/AMT.

12.4 Antiquity of World Civilizations

The chronology established in my previous books (Ramayana in 12209 BCE, Mahabharata in 5561 BCE) assert that the Indian civilization is the most ancient civilization in the world.

This book further corroborates assertion of 5561 BCE as the year of the Mahabharata war.

12.5 Ancient Sarasvati River

The success of a theory is to be gauged by the predictions it makes and how many of these predictions come out to be true.

My predictions for the historicity of the river Sarasvati, and her tributaries, are being validated by new research from the fields of hydrology, geology, climatology, geophysics and morphodynamics of rivers.

The story gets even better when we realize that, for the first time, this combined evidence has allowed us to firmly establish the chronology of the Rigveda!

The story begins with my original work on the chronology of the Mahabharata. In 2011 CE, I established 5561 BCE as the year of the Mahabharata war. The Mahabharata text has more than 100 references to river Sarasvati which enables us to ascertain the state of the river at the time of the Mahabharata. The river is described as flowing with ample water in many places. However, the river is also described as disappearing in the sands of the desert, flowing underground at other locations, and emerging from the sands at still other locations.

In, 2014 CE, I established 12209 BCE as the year of the Rama-Ravana yuddha. The Valmiki Ramayana descriptions tell us that the river Sarasvati was indeed flowing during Ramayana; however, river Yamuna had already separated from it, and interestingly, the river Shutudri (Sutlaj) was no longer flowing south to meet river Sarasvati, but rather was flowing westward. Thus, during the 13th millennium BCE itself, Sarasvati was deprived of the waters of the rivers Shutudri and Yamuna and that meant, the grand Sarasvati of Rigveda was no longer grand during Ramayana and Mahabharata times.

These textual descriptions of river Sarasvati, when combined with absolute chronology of the Ramayana in the 13th millennium BCE and the Mahabharata in 6th millennium BCE lead to the following predictions for river Sarasvati and her tributaries:

1. The grand Sarasvati of Rigveda existed only before 12,209 BCE.
2. The river Shutudri had stopped flowing southward and stopped meeting river Sarasvati sometime before 12,209 BCE.

The confirmation of these predictions were validated in November of 2017.

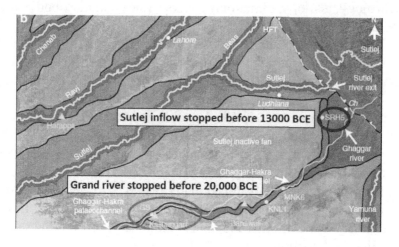

Singh (2017) showed that the river Shutudri had stopped flowing south, feeding its waters to river Sarasvati around 13,000 BCE. This was a phenomenal corroboration for the textual descriptions of the river Shutudri flowing west in 12,209 BCE (Ramayana times). This paper also showed, based on their analysis of earth cores obtained from the paleochannel of the river Sarasvati at Kalibangan, that the river Sarasvati had lost its "grand" status after 22,000 BCE. The implications of this study are staggering. This meant that the grand Sarasavati river, described in the oldest mandalas of Rigveda (6,3,7,4,2), existed only before 22,000 BCE, and that also meant these mandalas were composed before 22,000 BCE!

Let's turn to 6th millennium BCE, the timing of the Mahabharata. Although the Mahabharata text describes the river Sarasvati disappearing under the sand and flowing under the sand, numerous descriptions exist where river Sarasvati is flowing with ample lucid waters. And the natural question is if big rivers like Shutudri and Yamuna had stopped feeding waters to the river Sarasvati, long before 6th millennium BCE, what was the source of ample water in the river Sarasvati at the time of the Mahabharata war? The answer to this question came from climatology. Sarkar

(2016) showed decisive evidence for the intensification of monsoons beginning in 7000 BCE and lasting until 4500 BCE.

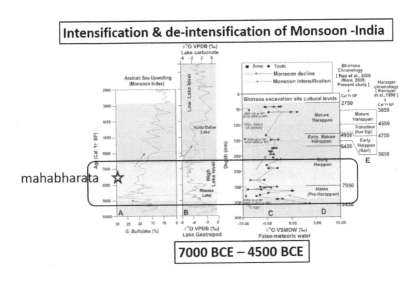

Thus, the evidence for the river Sarasvati corroborates the absolute chronology estimates of 5561 BCE for the Mahabharata and 12209 BCE for the Ramayana. And the additional benefit was the determination of the lower limit of 22,000 BCE for the composition of the oldest mandalas of the Rigveda (6,3,7,4,2).

12.6 Lower Limit on the Chronology of Rigveda

The oldest mandalas of the Rigveda (6,3,7) are predominantly composed by sages of Vasishtha and Vishwamitra lineages who were most active prior to and during the Ramayana times. The 10th and last mandala of the Rigveda contains richa that mention Rama, Vena, and Prithu of Ikshvaku lineage (10:93), and Shantanu and Devapi of Kuru lineage (10.98).

ऋषिः आर्तिषेणः देवापिः	छन्दः त्रिष्टुप्	देवता देवाः
बृहस्पते प्रति मे देवतामिहि मित्रो वा यदरुणो वासि पूषा		
आदित्यैर्वा यदसुभिरुरुत्वान्स पर्जन्यं शंतनवे वृषाय	॥ 1 ॥
आ देवो दूतो अजिरश्चिकित्वान्त्वद्देवापे अभि मार्मगच्छत्		
प्रतीचीनः प्रति मामा ववृत्स्व दधामि ते द्युमतीं वाचमासन्	॥ 2 ॥
अस्मे धेहि द्युमतीं वाचमासन्बृहस्पते अनमीवामिषिराम्		
ययौ वृष्टिं शंतनवे वनाव दिवो द्रप्सो मध्युमाँ आ विवेश	॥ 3 ॥
आ नो द्रप्सा मध्युमन्तो विशन्त्विन्द्र देह्यधिरथं सहस्रम्		
नि षीद होत्रमृतुथा यजस्व देवान्देवापे हविषा सपर्य	॥ 4 ॥
आर्तिषेणो होत्रमृषिर्निषीदन्देवापिर्देवसुमतिं चिकित्वान्		
स उत्तरस्मादधरं समुद्रमपो दिव्या असृजद्वर्ष्या अभि	॥ 5 ॥
अस्मिन्त्समुद्रे अध्युत्तरस्मिन्नापो देवेभिर्निवृता अतिष्ठन्		
ता अद्रवन्नार्तिषेणेन सृष्टा देवापिना प्रेषिता मृक्षिणीषु	॥ 6 ॥
यद्देवापिः शंतनवे पुरोहितो होत्राय वृतः कृपयन्नदीधेत्		
देवश्रुतं वृष्टिवनिं रराणो बृहस्पतिर्वाचमस्मा अयच्छत्	॥ 7 ॥
यं त्वा देवापिः शुशुचानो अग्न आर्तिषेणो मनुष्यः समीधे		
विश्वेभिर्देवैरनुमद्यमानः प्र पर्जन्यमीरया वृष्टिमन्तम्	॥ 8 ॥
त्वां पूर्व ऋषयो गीर्भिरायन्त्वामध्वरेषु पुरुहूत विश्वे		
सहस्राण्यधिरथान्यस्मे आ नो यज्ञं रोहिदश्वोप याहि	॥ 9 ॥
एतान्यग्ने नवतिर्नव त्वे आहुतान्यधिरथा सहस्रा		
तेभिर्वर्धस्व तन्वः शूर पूर्वीर्दिवो नो वृष्टिमिषितो रिरीहि	॥ 10 ॥
एतान्यग्ने नवति सहस्रा सं प्र यच्छ वृष्ण इन्द्राय भागम्		
विद्वान्पथ ऋतुशो देव्यानानप्यौलानं दिवि देवेषु धेहि	॥ 11 ॥
अग्ने बाधस्व वि मृधो वि दुर्गहापामीवामप रक्षांसि सेध		
अस्मात्समुद्राद्बृहतो दिवो नोऽपां भूमानमुप नः सृजेह	॥ 12 ॥

King Shantanu was the father of Bhishma, and one may wonder how this information became part of the Rigveda. The answer is rather easy. The Mahabharata text tells us that Maharshi Veda Vyasa did edit the Vedas.

Adi (CE 57:72-76, GP 63:87-91)

पादापसारिणं धर्मं विद्वान्स तु युगे युगे |
आयुः शक्तिं च मर्त्यानां युगानुगमवेक्ष्य च ॥७२॥

ब्रह्मणो ब्राह्मणानां च तथानुग्रहकाम्यया |
विव्यास वेदान्यस्माच्च तस्माद्व्यास इति स्मृतः ॥७३॥

208

वेदानध्यापयामास महाभारतपञ्चमान् ।
सुमन्तुं जैमिनिं पैलं शुकं चैव स्वमात्मजम् ॥७४॥

प्रभुर्वरिष्ठो वरदो वैशम्पायनमेव च ।
संहितास्तैः पृथक्त्वेन भारतस्य प्रकाशिताः ॥७५॥

तथा भीष्मः शान्तनवो गङ्गायाममितद्युतिः ।
वसुवीर्यात्समभवन्महावीर्यो महायशाः ॥७६॥

Thus, we can infer that the last (10th) mandala was edited during the Mahabharata times. This means that the 6th millennium BCE is the lower limit for the chronology of the Rigveda.

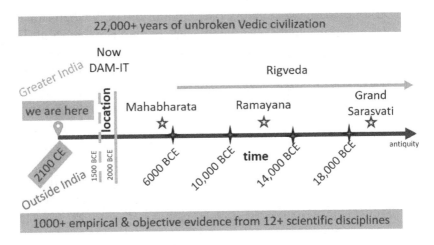

Now, DAM-IT refers to the "Now discredited Aryan migration/invasion theory."

12.7 Improving Quality of Indic Research

My original research work presented in this book, when combined with work presented in my previous two books, have huge implications for the quality of research being conducted in ancient Indian history.

My work has single-handedly shifted the research methodology away from dogmatic, skeptical, and manipulative methods to the most scientific method. In addition, the research presented in these three books not only meet but also exceed the requirements of 'sophisticated falsification' as explained by Imre Lakatos. Truthlikeness Score (TS) and Truthlikeness Method™ are tools to demonstrate aspects of 'sophisticated falsification'.

All Mahabharata researchers, barring a few notable exceptions such as S.B. Dikshit, P.V. Kane, and P.V. Vartak, have produced works that do not reach the level demanded by even a juvenile definition of falsification (e.g., dogmatic falsification). In fact, this is the very reason these researchers avoid discussion of any evidence that instantaneously falsify their claims.

12.8 Myth of a Theory That Explains Everything

If one dreams of a theory that explains not only when Bhishma-nirvana occurred but also the mystery behind Bhishma's ability to keep himself alive until the day of the winter solstice, we certainly cannot blame such an individual. We all would want to see such a theory.

In scientific language, we will call such a theory, a theory with the highest level of universality. Why don't we have such theories in physics, chemistry, biology, evolution, geology, genetics, or history? The reason we don't have such theories with a high level of universality is because such theories are too far removed from the level reached by the testable science of the day and for that very reason may give rise to a metaphysical system.

12.9 Path of Science

One who truly understands this scientific process will immediately recognize that the merit of a specific theory is always to be judged in the context of another theory, whether one's own or those of others. Discussion of a theory in the absence of another theory or without the context of a specific problem is futile. This is because science is not a system of certain well-established statements, nor is it a system that steadily advances towards a state of

210

finality. Although it can neither attain truth nor probability, the striving for knowledge and the search for truth are still the strongest motives for scientific discovery.

Not all poetry is mythical and not all science is cosmology. And it is not unusual to see poetry and science come together when one reads Nasadiya sukta of Rigveda. A large part not only of poetry but also of sciene can still be described as naïve attempts, of explaining our world to ourselves.

Bold ideas, unjustified anticipations, and speculative thoughts are our only means for interpreting nature and history. We must hazard them to win our prize. As Novalis said, "Theories are like nets; those who cast may catch." Oscar Wilde says, "Experience is the name everyone gives to their mistakes," and John Archibald Wheeler says, "Our whole problem is to make the mistakes as fast as possible." Those among us who are unwilling to expose their ideas to the hazard of refutation do not take part in the scientific game.

Selected Bibliography

1. The Mahabharata (CE). BORI critical edition. Bhandarkar Oriental Research Institute, Pune.
2. The Mahabharata (GP) – Gita press edition with Sanskrit text and Hindi translation. Gita Press, Gorakhpur, India.
3. The Mahabharata (SR) – Southern recension (1934), critically edited by P S Sastri. V Ramaswamy Sastrulu & Sons. Madras, India.
4. Oak, Nilesh (2011) When did the Mahabharata war happen? : The Mystery of Arundhati. Danphe Inc., USA.
5. Popper, Karl (2002) Conjectures and Refutations, Routledge, London, UK.
6. Popper, Karl (2002) The Logic of Scientific Discovery, Routledge, London, UK.
7. Rigveda Samhita, Gita Press, Gorakhapur, U.P. India.
8. Sarkar et al (2016) Oxygen isotope in archaeological bio-apatites from India: Implications to climate change and decline of Bronze Age Harappan civilization, Scientific Reports, 6:26555, DOI: 10:1038/srep26555
9. Singh et al (2017) Counter-intuitive influence of Himalayan river morphodynamics on Indus Civilisation urban settlements, Nature Communications, 8:1617, DOI: 10.1038/s41467-017-01643-9
10. Talageri, Shrikant (2000) The Rigveda – A Historical Analysis, Aditya Prakashan, New Delhi, India.

About the Author

Nilesh helps Indians become aware of the deep antiquity of Indian civilization so that they truly comprehend, present or defend the grand narrative of India unlike most other Indic researchers because he builds it through scientific acumen and logical reasoning.

Nilesh is the author of "When did the Mahabharata War Happen? The Mystery of Arundhati" (2011) and "The Historic Rama: Indian Civilization at the End of Pleistocene" (2014), where he freshly evaluated astronomy observations of the Mahabharata and the Ramayana. His work led to the validation of 5561 BCE as the year of the Mahabharata war and 12209 BCE as the year of Rama-Ravana Yuddha.

His first book was nominated for the **Lakatos Award**, which is given annually by the London School of Economics for a contribution to the philosophy of science.

Nilesh researches in astronomy, archaeology, anthropology, quantum mechanics, economics, ancient narratives, and philosophy.

Nilesh's writes on "Ancient Indian History" through his blog at: http://nileshoak.wordpress.com/

Made in the USA
Columbia, SC
18 February 2021

33211194R00124